Old Carse of Gowrie – West
with Kinfauns, Glencarse, Errol and Rait
Alan Brotchie

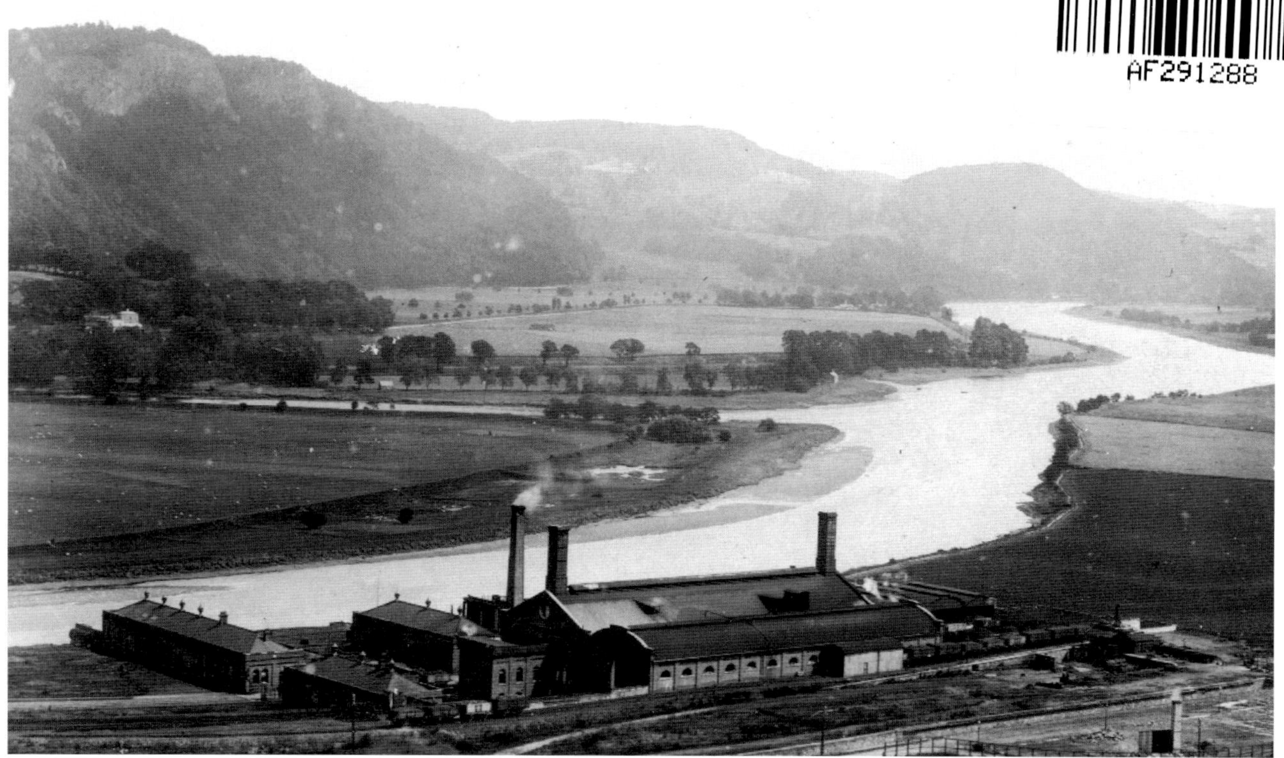

Looking east from the Edinburgh road across the westernmost part of the Carse, the downstream end of Moncrieff or Friarton Island on the left. On the island is the King James VI Golf Course, designed by Tom Morris Senior and named after the king who is said to have played on the North Inch where the club had its original home. The Tay divides round the island with the main channel closest to the camera serving the harbour. The lesser channel to the north, the so-called Willowgate, rejoins at the centre of this scene. Moncrieff Island is very much more overgrown today, while the industrial use of the south bank of the river extends much further east. The new Friarton Bridge now dominates the entire vista.

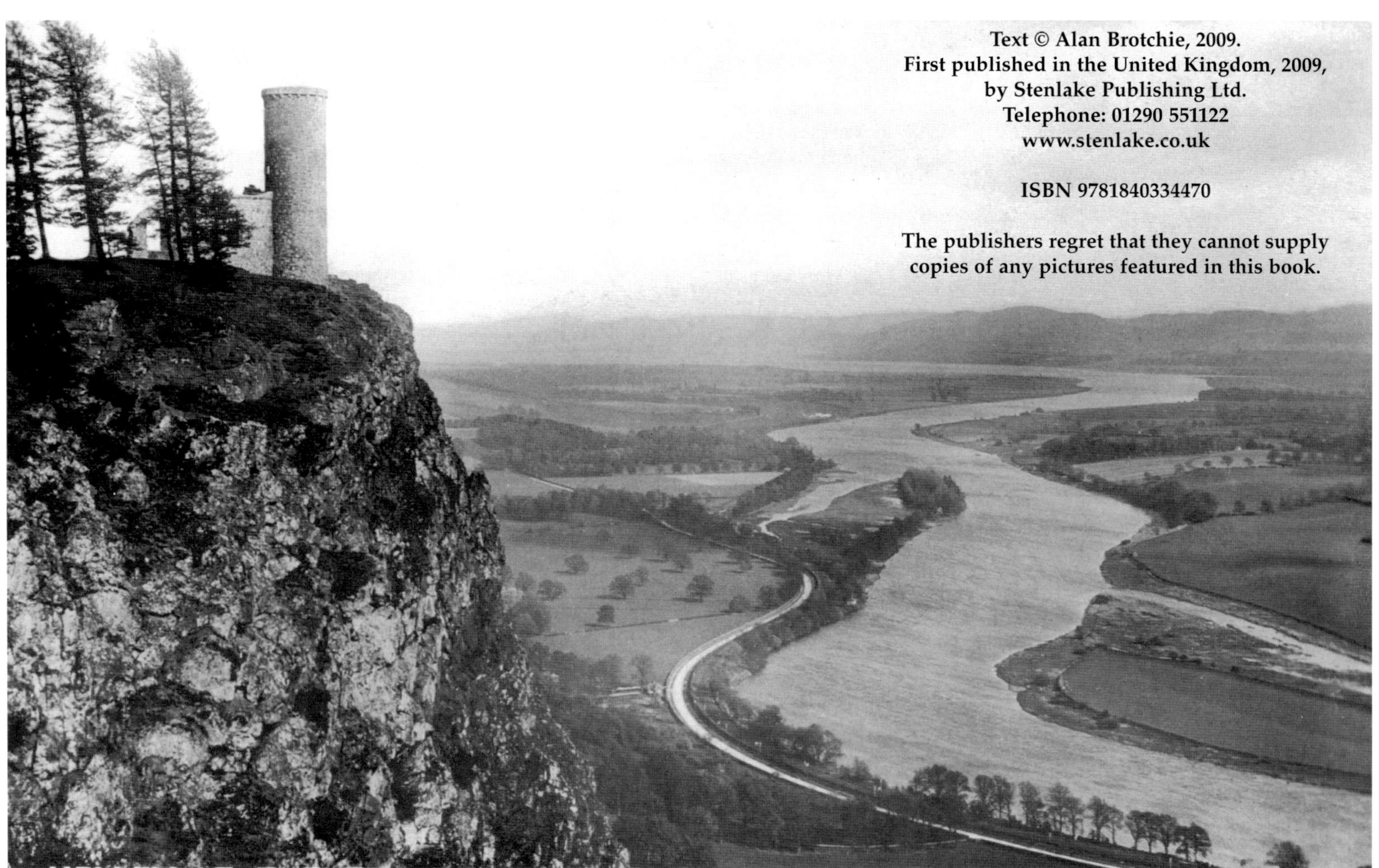

Text © Alan Brotchie, 2009.
First published in the United Kingdom, 2009,
by Stenlake Publishing Ltd.
Telephone: 01290 551122
www.stenlake.co.uk

ISBN 9781840334470

The tower at the top of Kinnoull Hill dates from 1829 and was built as a 'folly' by the tenth Earl of Kinnoull to make the appearance of the site appeal more to his ideal image of the gorge of the Rhine with its romantic castles. The 729ft high prominence above the cliffs and the surrounding policies was purchased by Lord Dewar and handed to the city for the benefit of its inhabitants at a ceremony on 10th September 1924. On the right is Sleepless Inch, an isthmus into the river, probably an island in the not too distant past. The lodge of Kinfauns Castle is on the left of the first bend of the sweeping Perth to Dundee turnpike road.

     Kinnoull Hill

INTRODUCTION

'The Fruitful Valley' – an epithet given to the Carse of Gowrie many years ago, has never been more appropriate than today. The name is applied to a level area of alluvial ground some twenty miles long and five miles wide at its broadest. Scotland's most fertile plain, lying between the Sidlaw Hills and the River Tay, was for centuries a treacherous morass. The glens which cross northwards through the hills to Strathmore – known as 'glacks' – were all guarded, some by a castle at both ends. Down each glack ran (and still runs) a burn usually supporting a small village at its southern end. Each settlement had its complement of smiddy, church, cotter houses, joiner, etc. and each enjoyed stunning southerly views over the Carse to the river and the hills of north Fife beyond. These attributes have in recent years brought changes to the character of these hamlets, many homes now the haunt of motorised commuters who work in Perth, Dundee or even further afield.

The settlements within the Carse proper tended to cling to the few slight eminences which kept above flood water level, the self-proclaimed 'Capital of the Carse' being the village of Errol. Not until 1735 was land improvement on any scale commenced (by Hay of Leys by Errol), a project which was advanced with enthusiasm by John Lee Allen of Errol Park a hundred years later. He reclaimed 100 acres from the river, was responsible for construction of flood restraining embankments, planted reed beds to stabilise the river edge and improved drainage. He was also responsible for the establishment of brick and tile works to provide the fundamentals necessary for improvement. Change was in the air, with construction (started 1790) of the turnpike road up through the centre of the Carse with subsidiary roads running from it at right angles. Railways followed, the Perth to Dundee line opened in 1847, changing the nature of transport in the area. Further recent changes have seen the improvement of the complete length of the Carse spine road , the A90. Speeding motorists can let their eyes wander for just a few seconds to appreciate the unchanging beauty of the landscape through which they are passing. That said, while the landscape itself does not change, there are many changes visible in the manner farming is now conducted. Much of the Carse, where for generations soft fruit and berries have been traditionally grown, have seen plastic poly tunnels take the place of nature. Crops may have become more profitable, but the aesthetics of Scotland's showcase landscape have been compromised severely in the process.

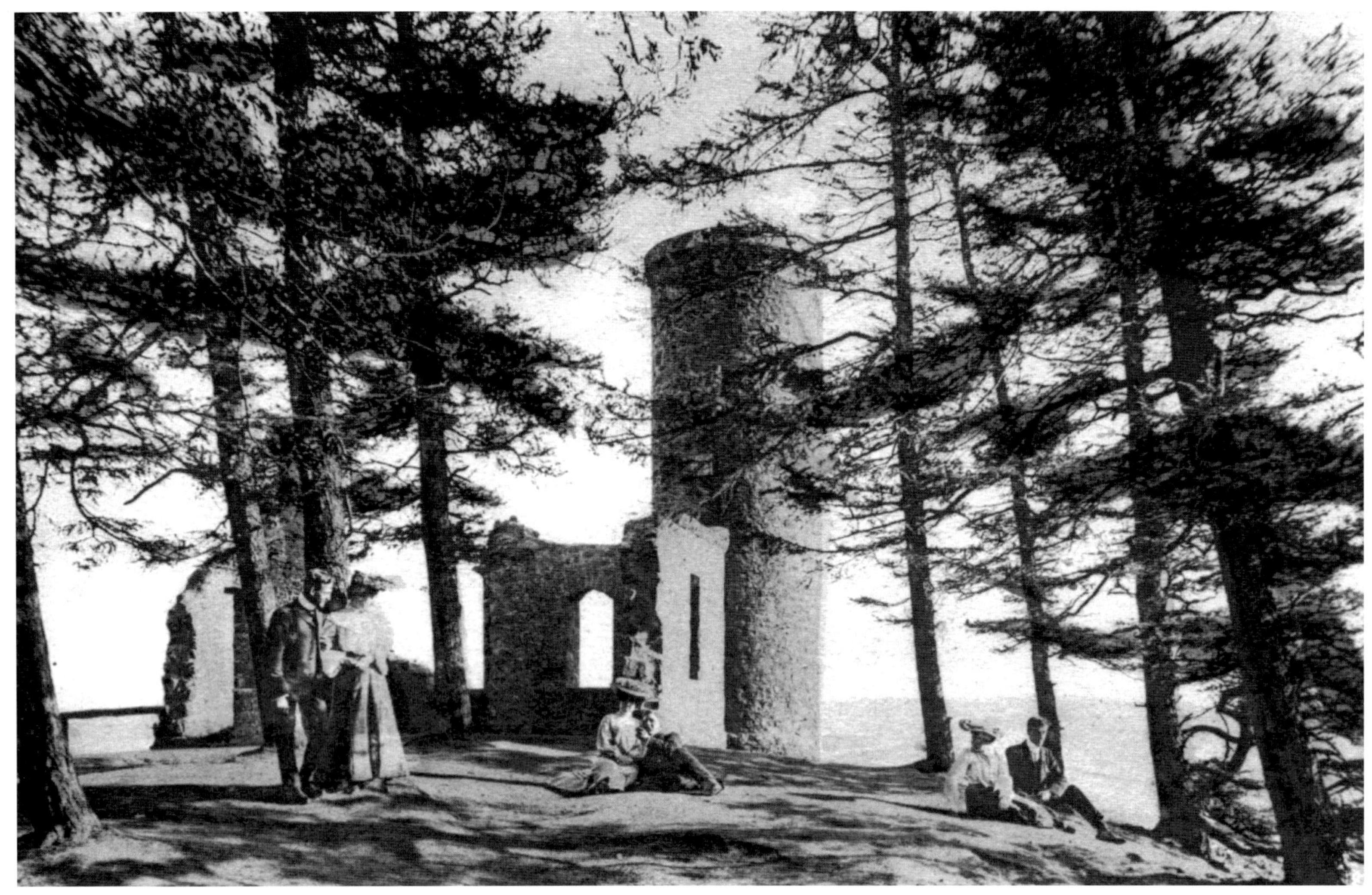

The 'ruins' at the summit of Kinnoull Hill were a popular trysting place, and the climb is still a very popular mature woodland walk. The serenity of the spot now has to compete with the constant intrusion of road traffic noise from the A90. Just below the summit is a cave known as the Dragon's Den, where a King of the Picts is reputed to have killed a great monster to show his esteem for St Serf!

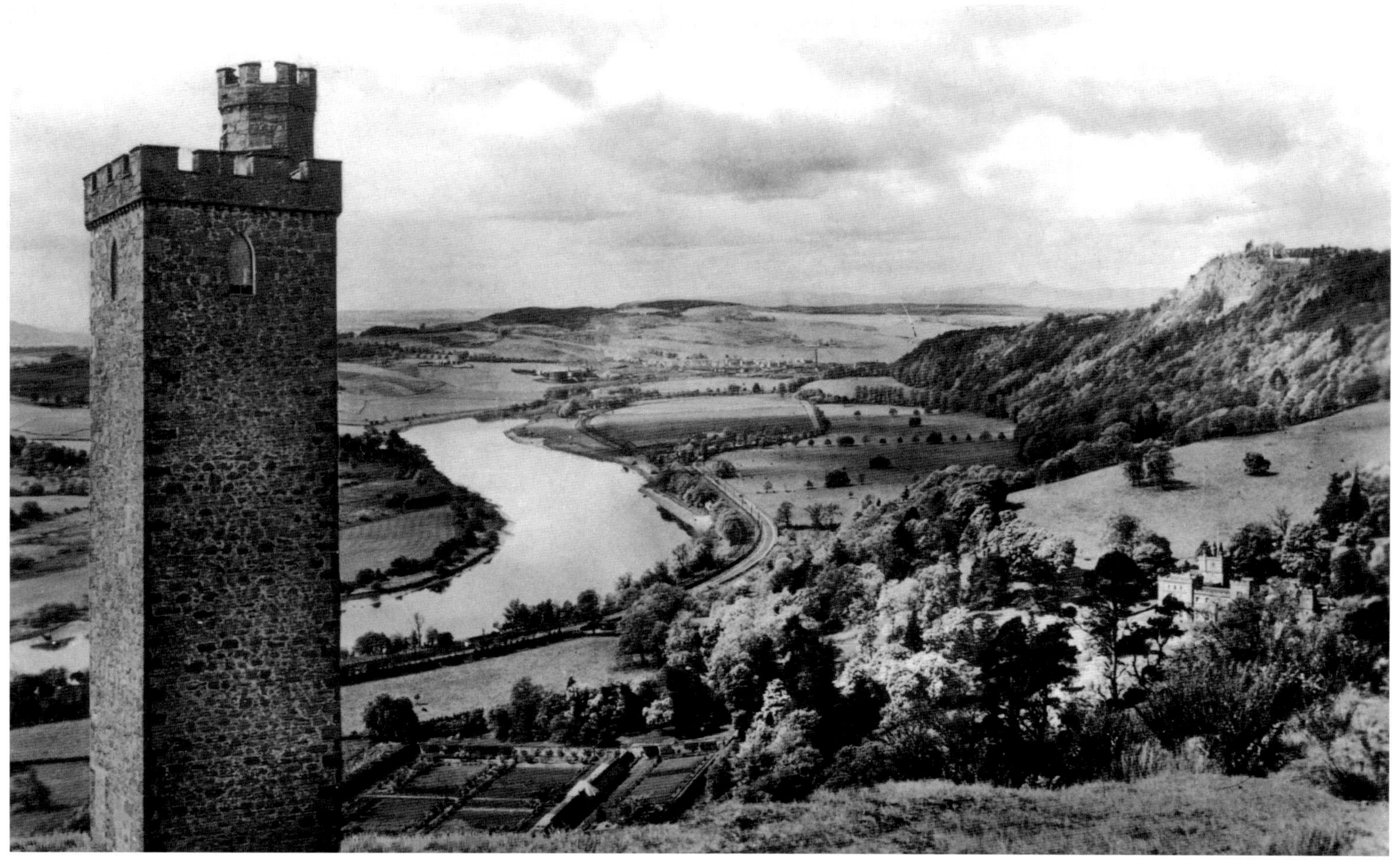

On top of Binn Hill overlooking the river, slightly lower in elevation than Kinnoull at 555ft height, the first addition to the works of nature was this observatory tower built about 1816 to the instructions of the fourteenth Lord Gray of Kinfauns. This entire area, encompassing five summits (Binn, Kinnoull, Corsiehill, Barnhill and Deuchray), is now a woodland park open to all and managed by the Forestry Commission. The view looking west has changed radically with the construction in 1975-1978 of the concrete Friarton Bridge linking the north end of the M90 to the Perth to Dundee road. As the tidal harbour at Perth is still operational the bridge, at 25 metres above water level, was designed to allow safe passage of vessels below. The associated approach and slip roads cover a significant area of prime agricultural land. In the foreground can be seen Kinfauns Castle and its walled garden.

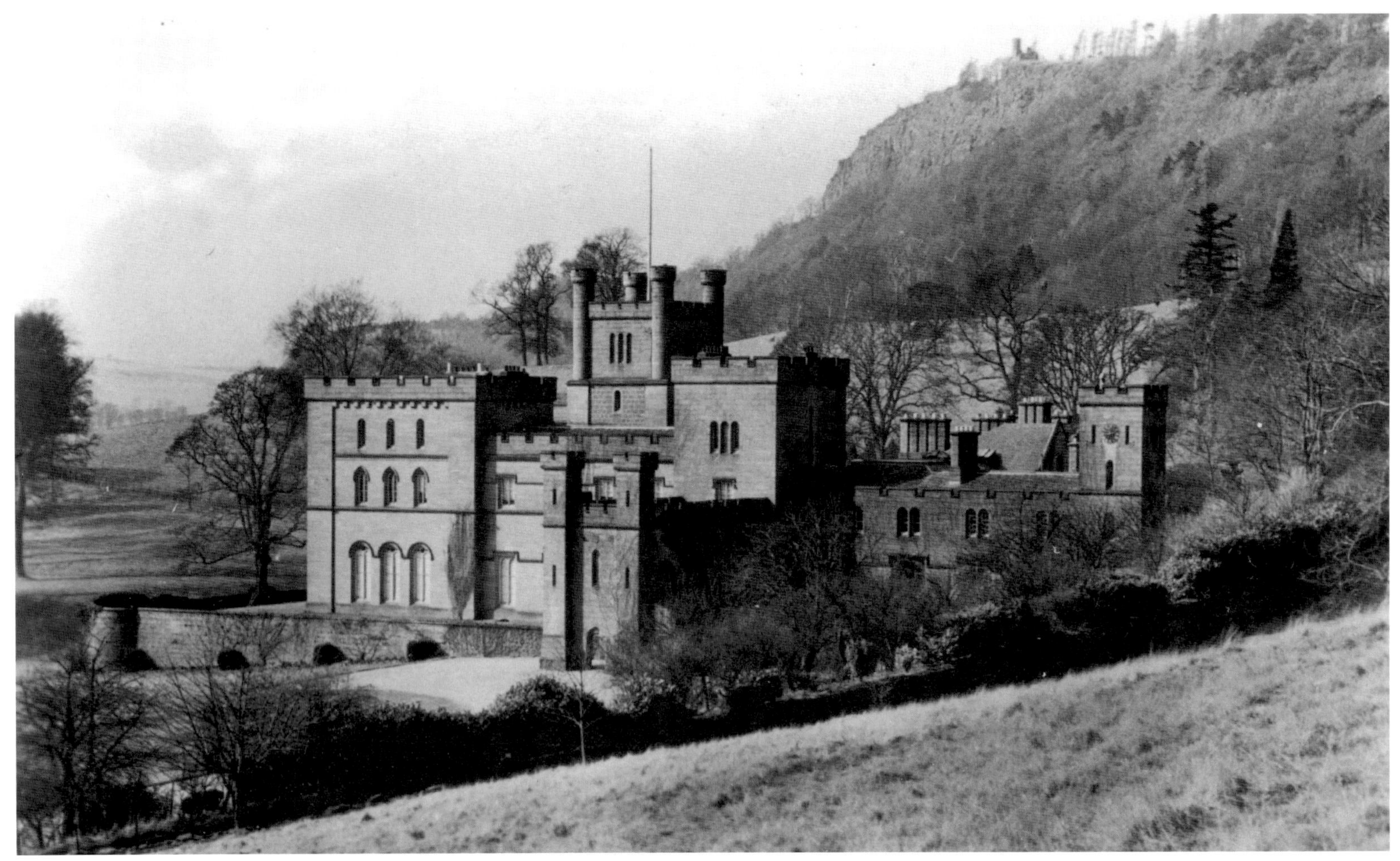

Kinfauns Castle was constructed in the 1820s for Lord Gray on a spectacular site above the river. Designed by the highly acclaimed architect Sir Robert Smirke, the Home Farm was designed by the perhaps even better known Sir Robert Lorimer. The castle has been described as one of Smirke's 'romantic gothic confections'. Having changed hands and uses several times, since July 2004 the castle has been one of the homes of Mrs Ann Gloag OBE who, with her brother Brian Souter, founded the Stagecoach bus group in 1980. Much controversy was occasioned following erection of a high perimeter security fence round part of the estate, but its continued existence was confirmed following legal action.

     Kinfauns Castle

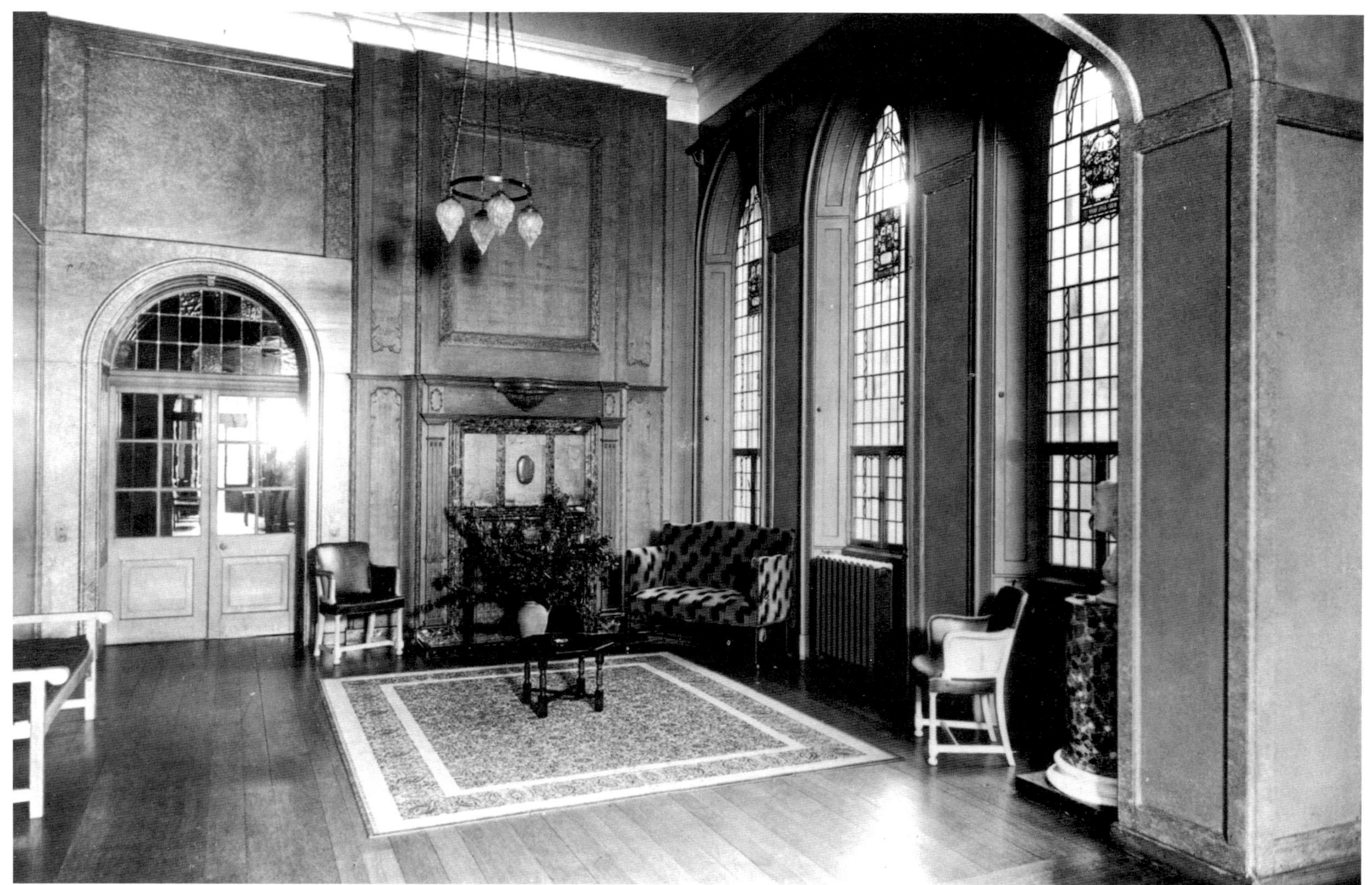

Original features of the A-listed building included William Morris designed wallpaper. Prior to Mrs Gloag's ownership the castle had been transformed for a relatively brief life as an upmarket hotel by James Smith, former chief executive in Hong Kong for Hilton Asia. This earlier view of the old billiard room shows the three arched windows, each framing a piece of early seventeenth century German stained glass work.

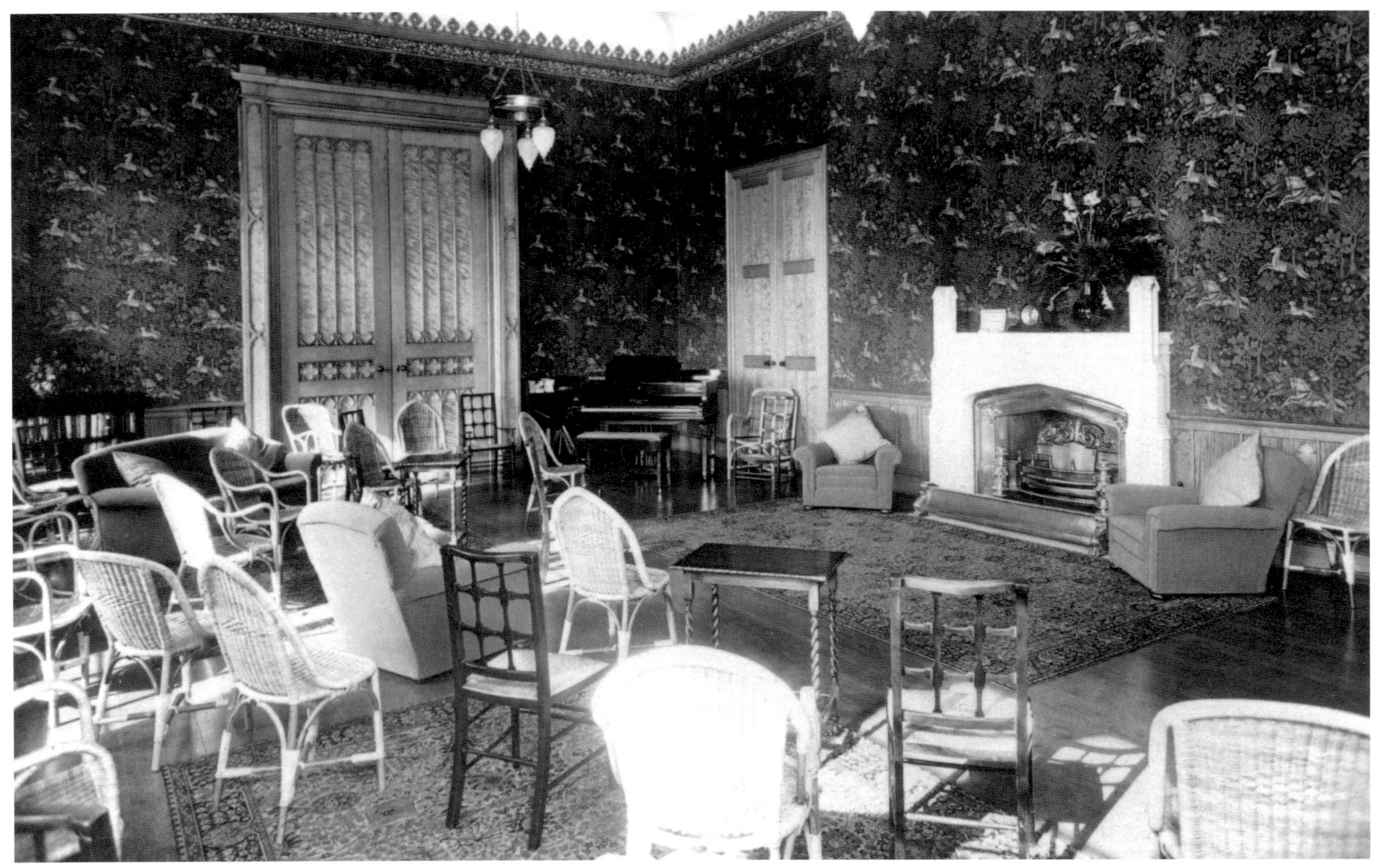

Prior to its life as an hotel, the building was used for many years as a holiday home by the Cooperative Holiday Association (CHA) as a centre for walking holidays. It is only to be hoped that the holidaymakers appreciated their sumptuous surroundings! This spectacular room, used by the CHA as their Common Room, was previously the 'large drawing room', complete with white marble fireplace, specially designed wallpaper and ornate cornices. Adjoining this was the 82 feet long gallery, used to display Baron Gray's portraiture and other family treasures.

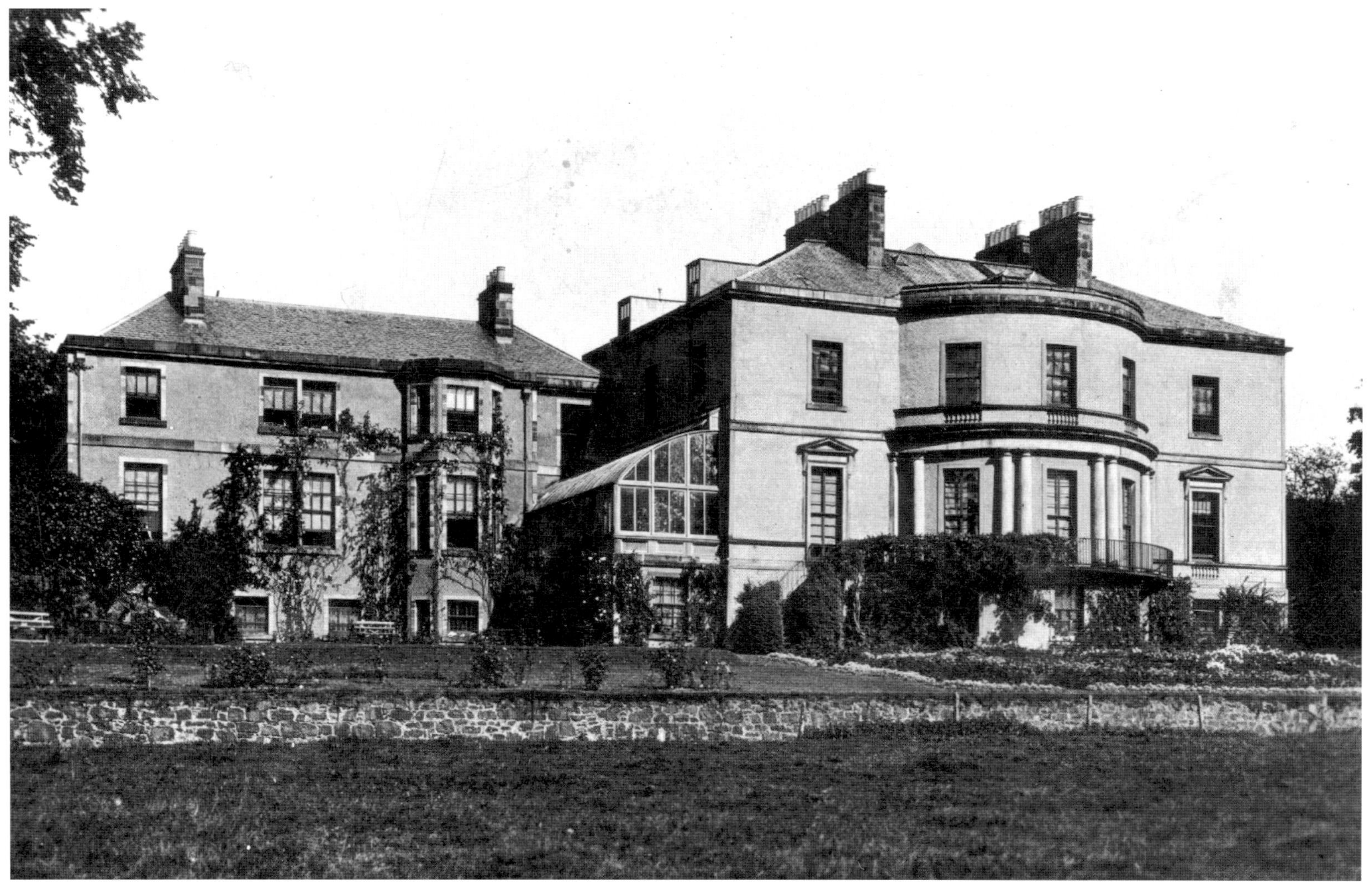

Seggieden House was demolished in the 1970s, having stood derelict for many years following major fire damage. A loss to the local architectural scene, it was designed by John Paterson, who also was responsible for many other local mansions. The building contained several well-proportioned oval-shaped rooms. Close by is its still extant ice house, then much used to preserve salmon from the Kinfauns beat.

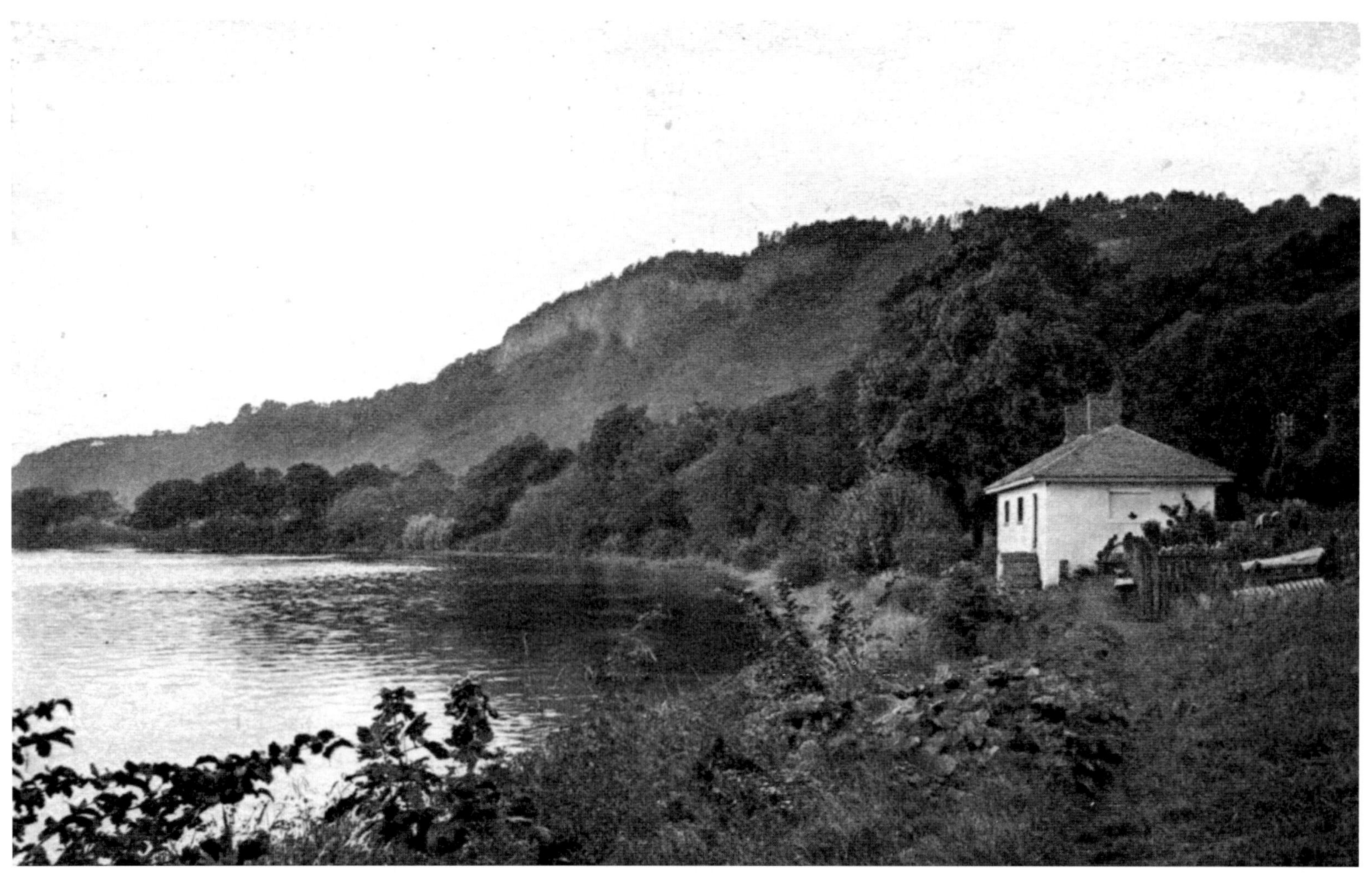

Kinfauns salmon fishers' bothy with Kinnoull Hill behind. When the Perth to Dundee railway was constructed in 1847 the bothys were cut off from easy access to the main road. To overcome the problem of movement of boxes of fish, most were provided with short lengths of narrow gauge railway, the entire rolling stock consisting normally of just one flat bed trolley per line! Each fishing beat was known by its distinctive name, there being, amongst others, the Flukie, Venture, Skin the Goat, Haggis, Eppie's Taes, etc.

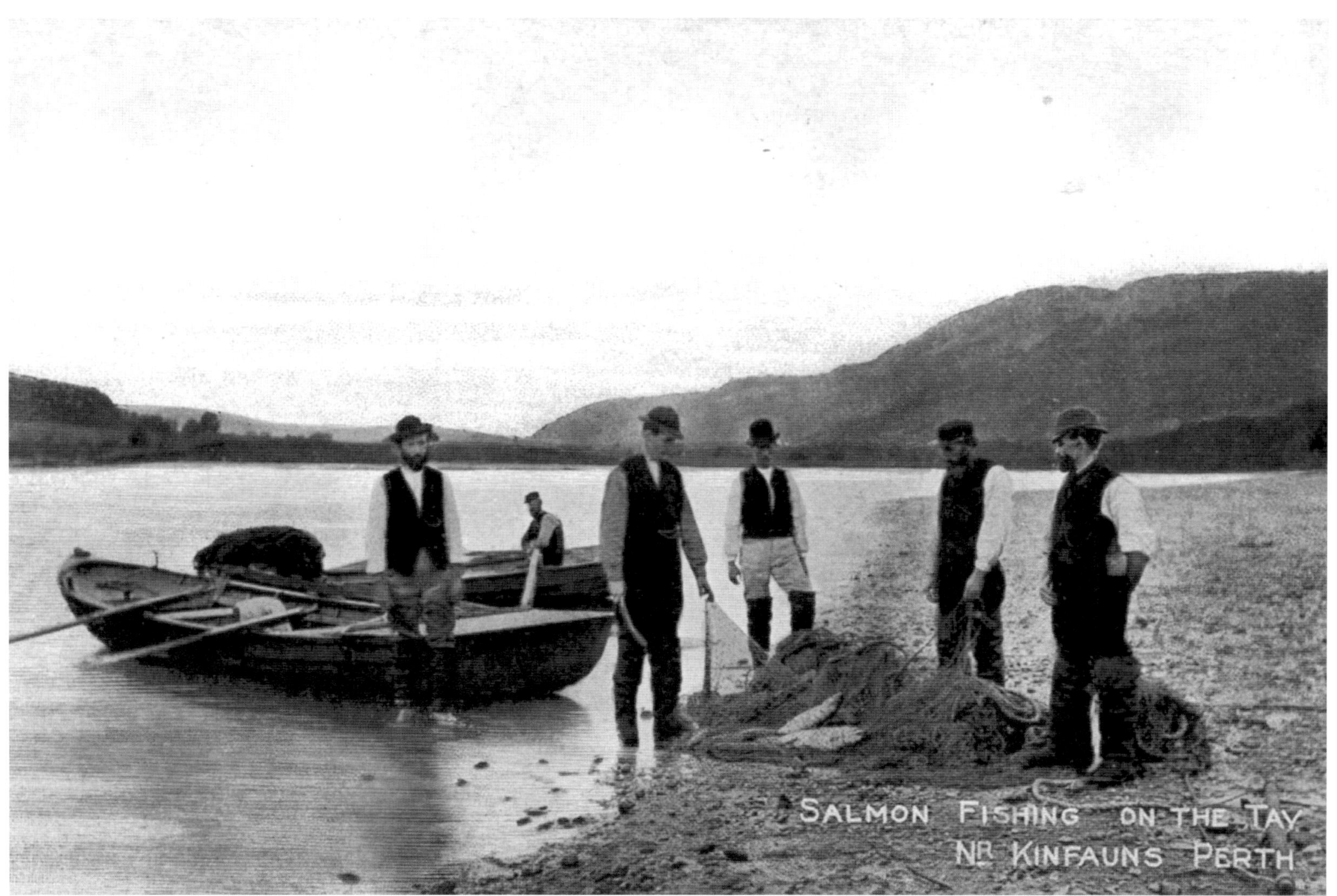

A goodly haul from the Tay at Kinfauns beat. The fisherman third from the left has the 'priest' in his right hand, used with great effect to despatch the caught fish. One sharp blow to the vital point behind the head was all that was necessary.

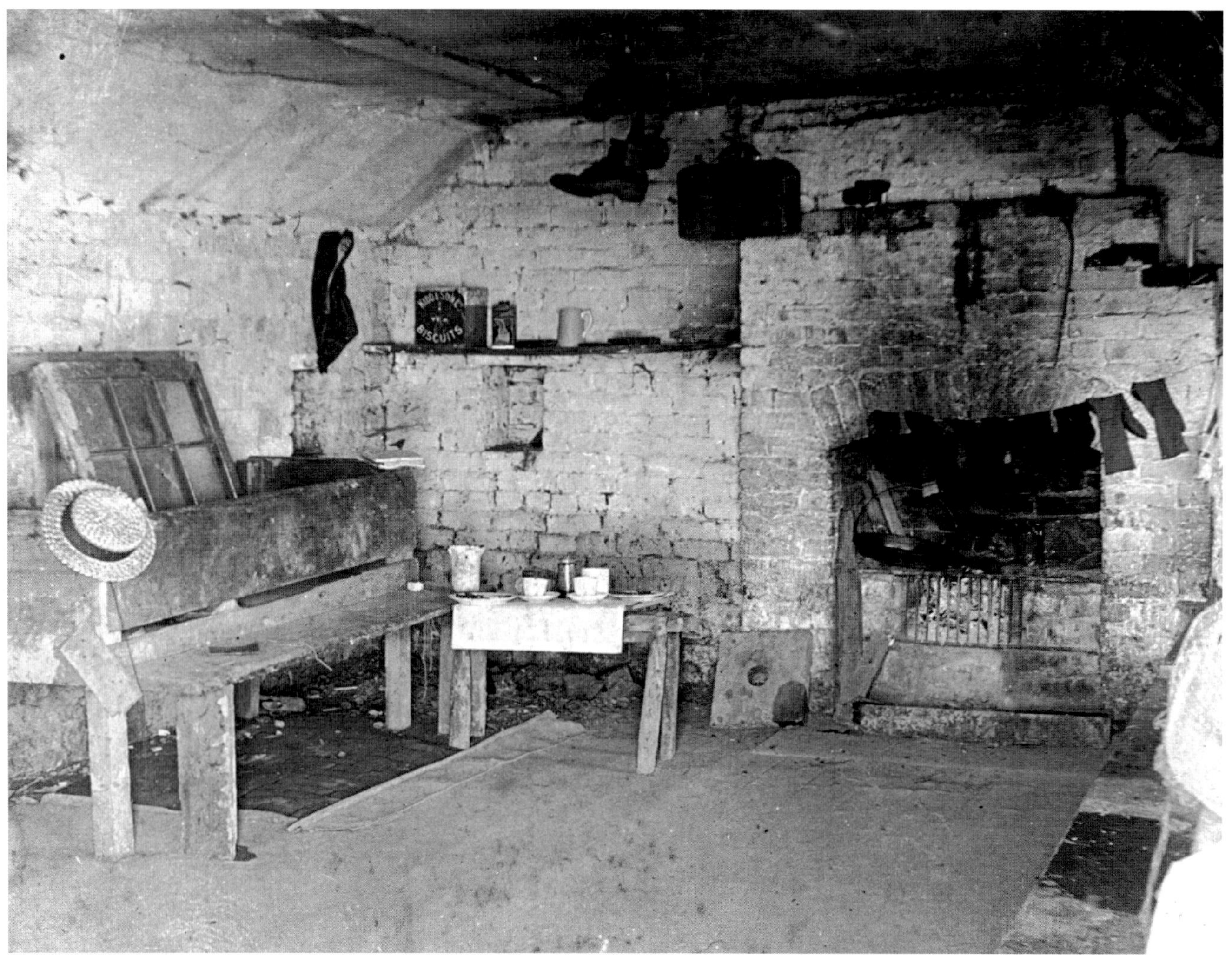

Home comforts in one of the River Tay salmon bothys. During the season a bothy would be home to six to eight men. Although basic in the extreme, it probably was not much different from the typical farm workers' lodging at the end of the nineteenth century. The tablecloth is a newspaper, socks dry by the fireside and boots hang from the ceiling. The 'boater' on the box-bed is unlikely gear for a fisherman, and probably belonged to the photographer.

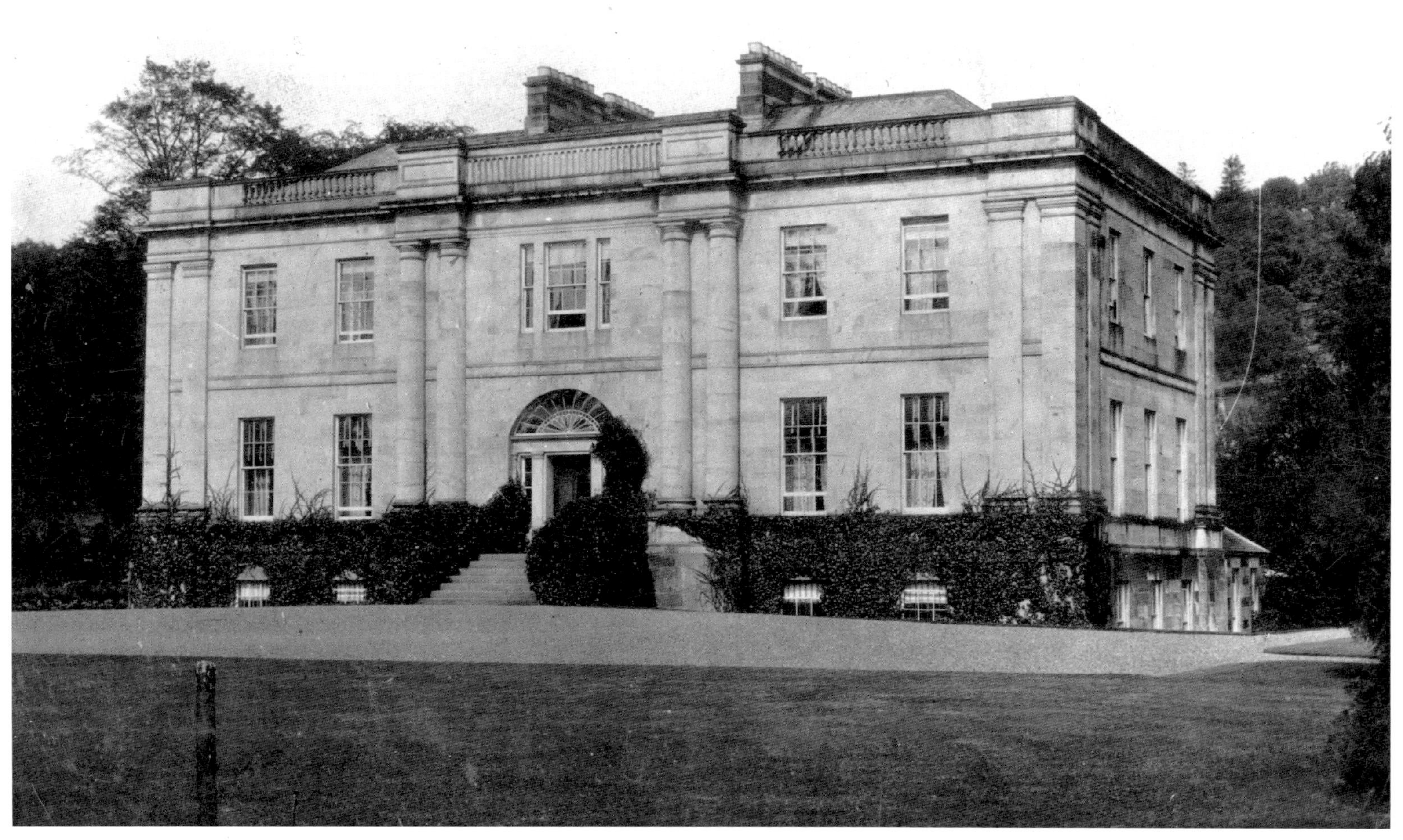

Inchyra House is a remarkably bold mansion constructed about 1810 west of Glencarse to the order of a successful Edinburgh legal luminary, John Anderson. A Victorian gazetteer advises 'Inchyra has a good harbour which admits vessels of considerable burden, and a ferry communicating with Fingask in Rhynd parish'. The small harbour at Inchyra was, by the eighteenth century, heavily involved in export of agricultural produce.

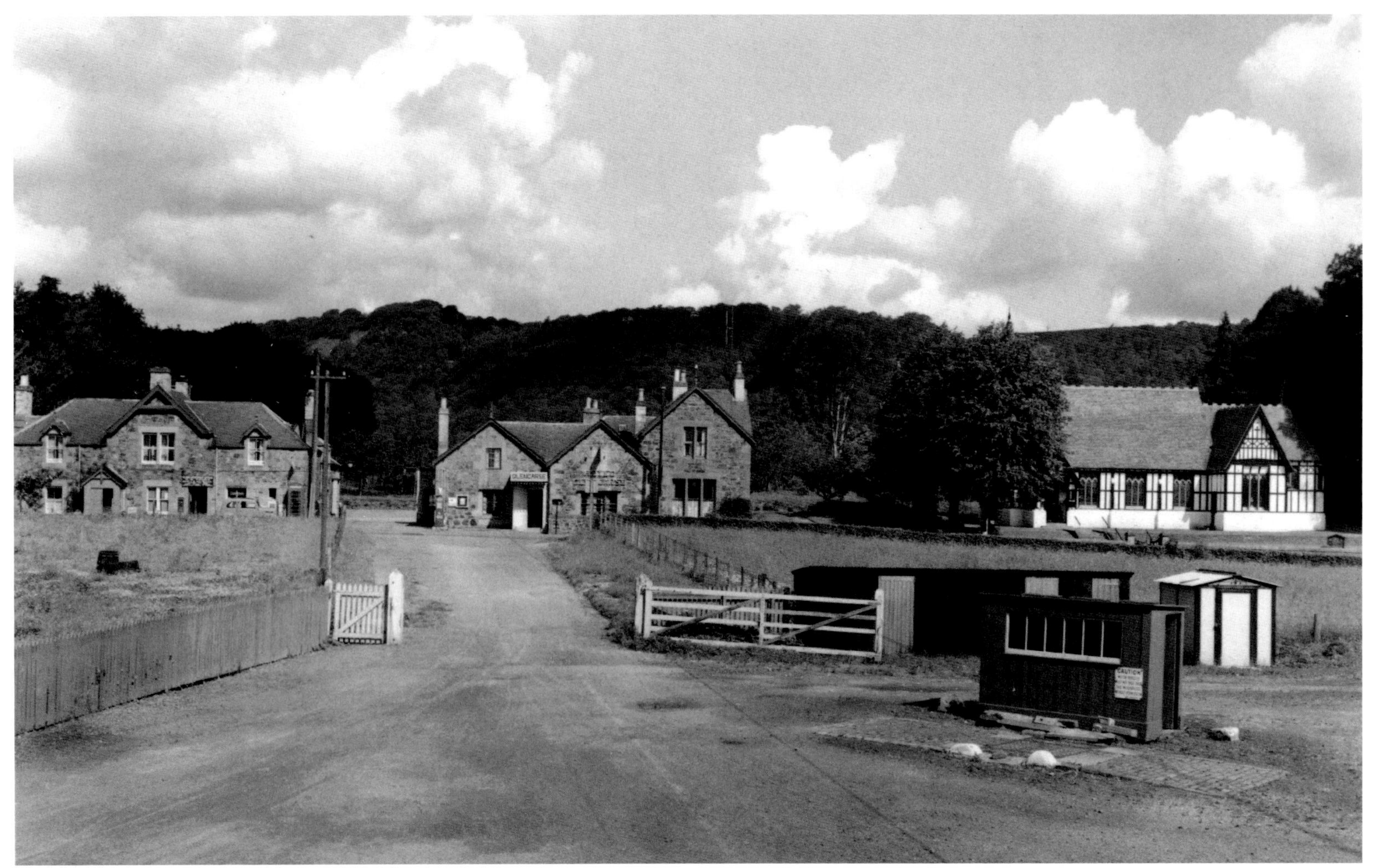

The view greeting a traveller arriving at Glencarse Station in 1956; trains still run, but now pass without stopping. Passenger services were withdrawn from 11th June of that year, goods trains continued to use the yard until November 1964. Today the dual carriageway cuts between the railway and the village. To the right can be seen the distinctive half-timbered All Saints Episcopal Church, built in 1878 from 'pitch pine and concrete'. Note the weighbridge in the station yard.

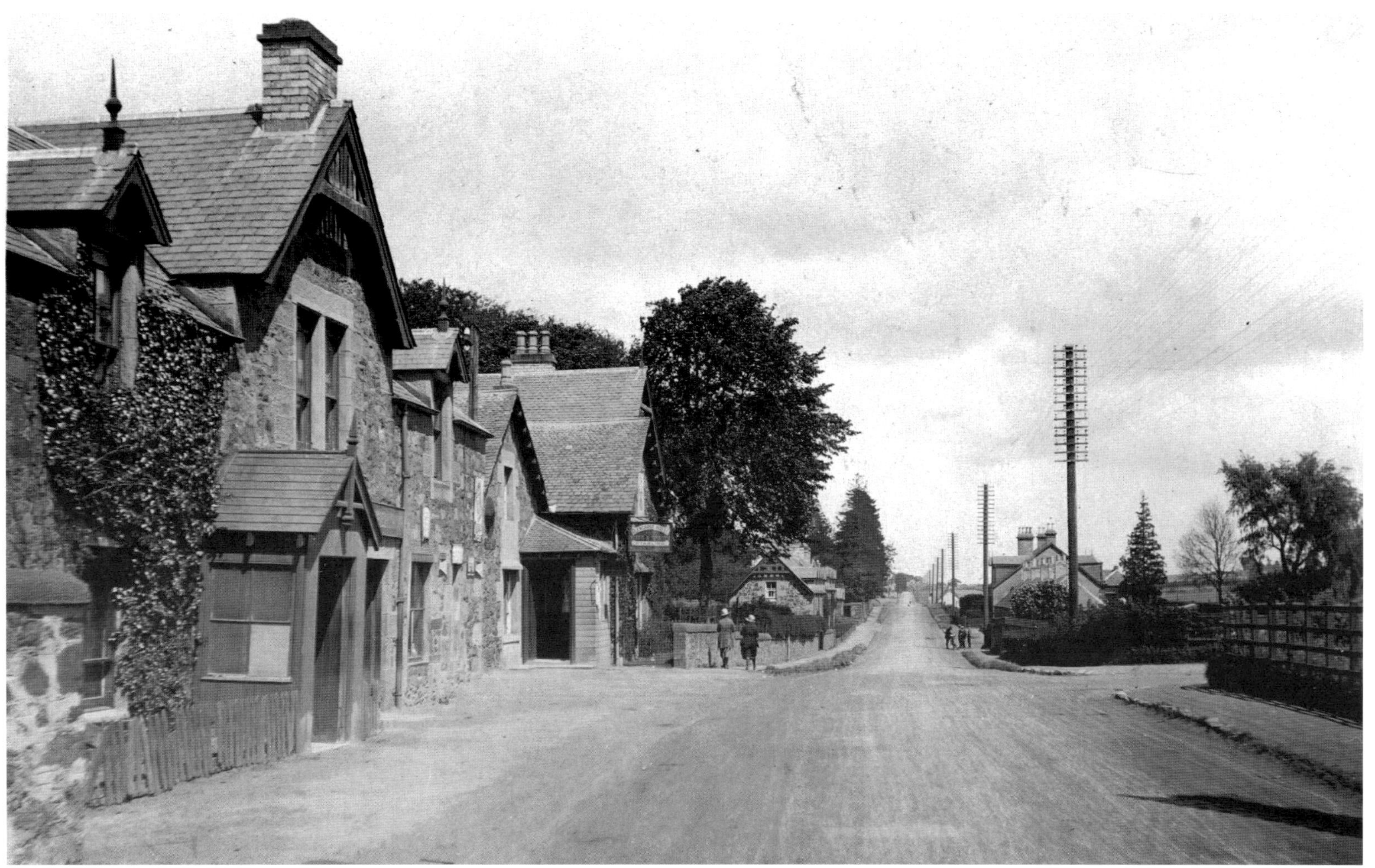

Much of the original estate village Newtown of Glencarse dated from the eighteenth century. This deserted scene in Glencarse with a totally traffic-free main road to Dundee probably dates from the early 1920s, with the station entrance on the right, and buildings on the left which can be distinguished, unchanged, in the previous photograph. The first of these is the Post Office, then the Glencarse Hotel, originally a coaching Inn, and then a popular watering place in the days of the 'bona-fide traveller', when Sunday opening of a hotel bar was only to service those 'in transit' ,a much abused restriction!

Behind the Glencarse Hotel were stables and a smithy which, while serving the local farming community until the advent of World War 2, also serviced the growing automobile trade. Here is Will Ford, a well-known local worthy, posing in front of a vehicle whose BH 995 registration (confirmed from another photograph) proclaims it to have been registered initially in Buckinghamshire. This is quite remarkable, since the handsome vehicle is considered to be one of a limited number of 'Atholl' cars built by Angus Murray & Sons at the Craigton Engine Works in Govan in the period 1907-1908. While the registration details for Buckinghamshire mostly still exist, regrettably the only missing volume is that for April 1907 to May 1911 from which the details of this fascinating vehicle would have been uncovered. It appears to have been used as a taxi.

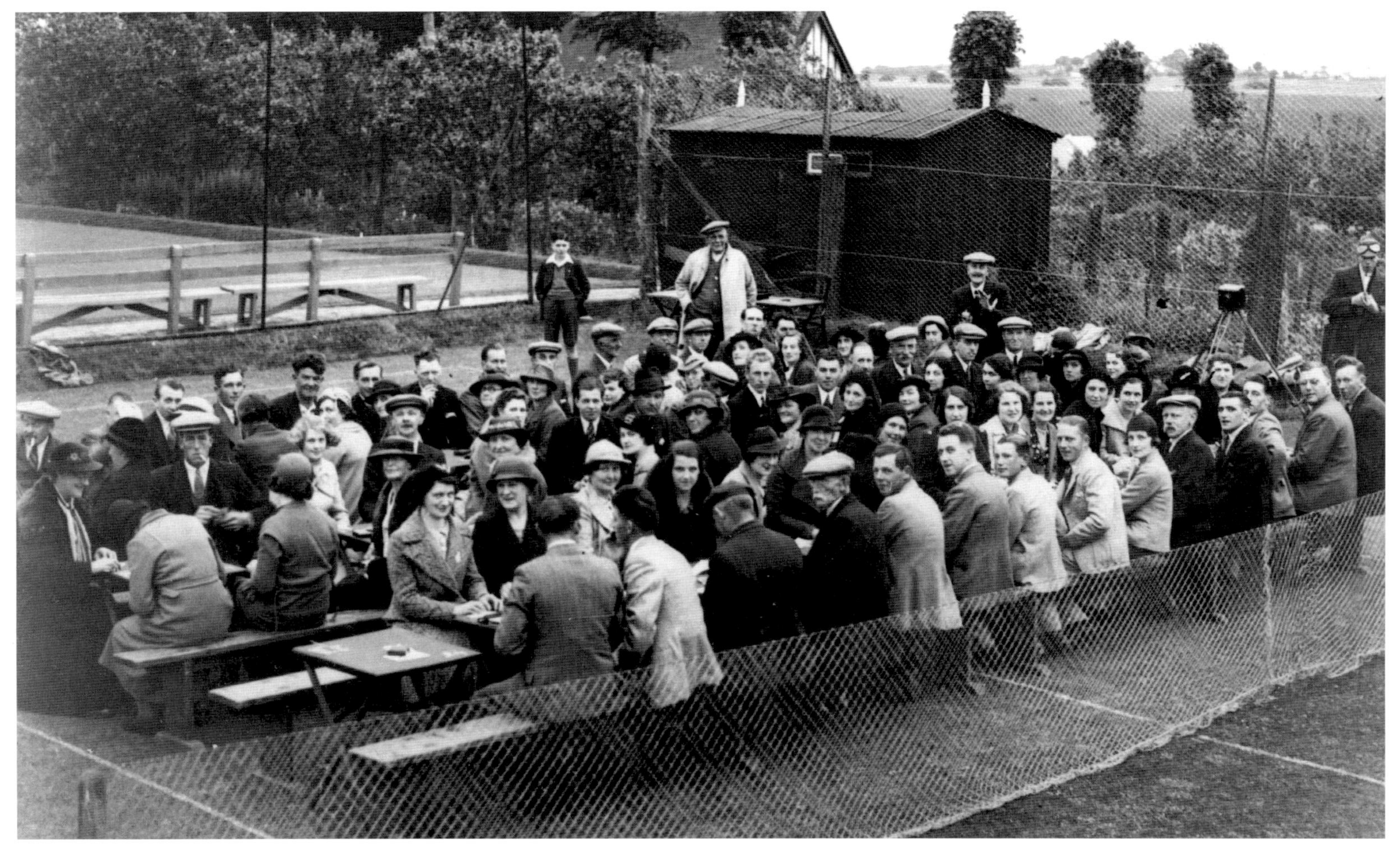

The bowling club at Glencarse was situated behind the hotel, where this open-air whist drive was held in 1930. Just discernable above the bowlers' hut is the top of the gable end of the black and white Episcopal Church. In the distance is Pitcoag Farm, by whose entrance can be found the 'Hawkstone'. The legend tells that these lands were granted by the king to the Hays of Errol where a falcon, released from Kinnoull Hill, first touched the ground.

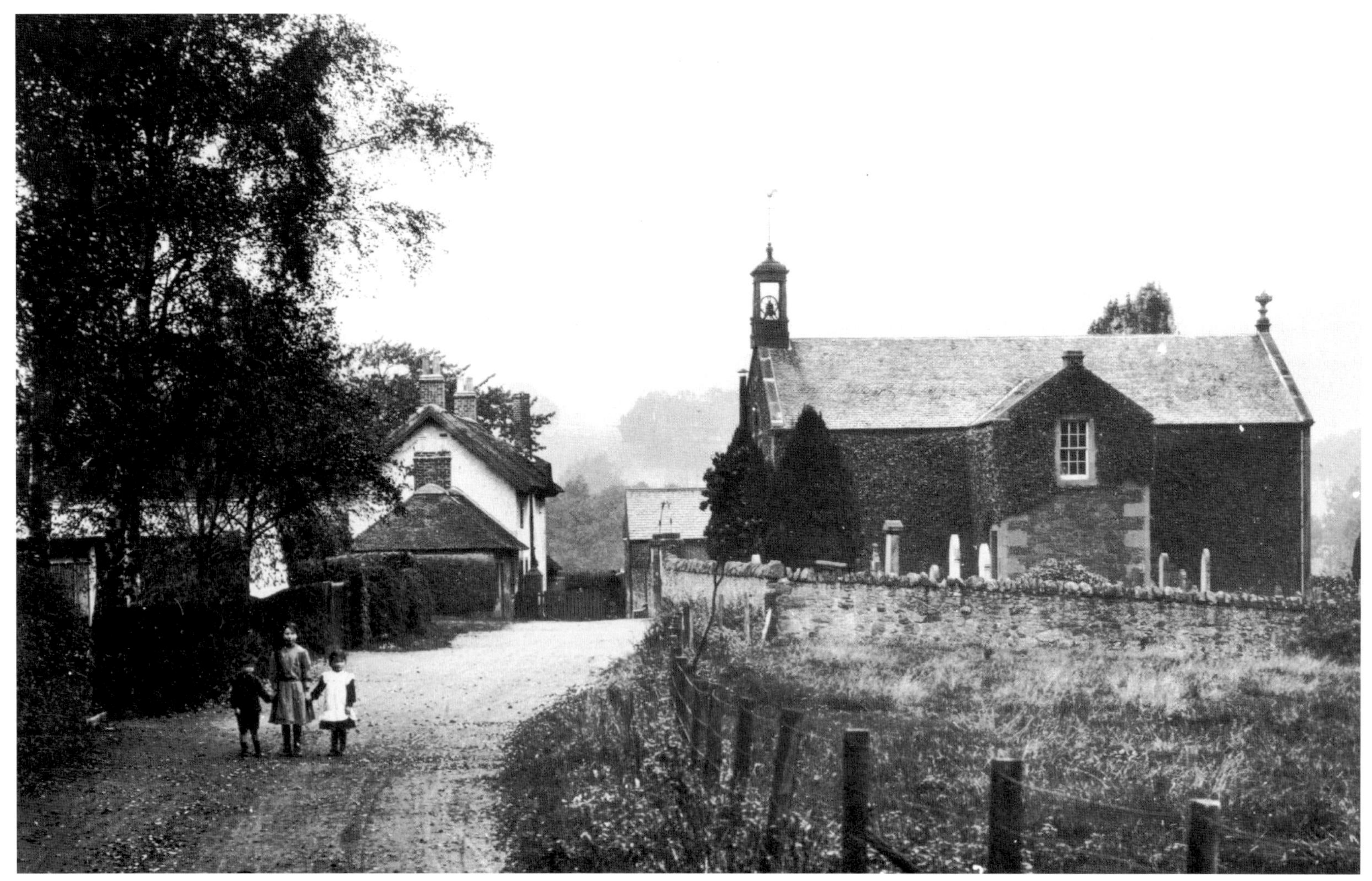

St. Madoes Parish encompasses the villages of Glencarse, Cottown and Leetown with a parish church dating from 1798 - 1799. The name is most frequently associated with the magnificent seven foot high Pictish carved stone dating to the eighth century which was formerly to be found in the churchyard. It has been removed for protection from the elements and is now in Perth Museum.

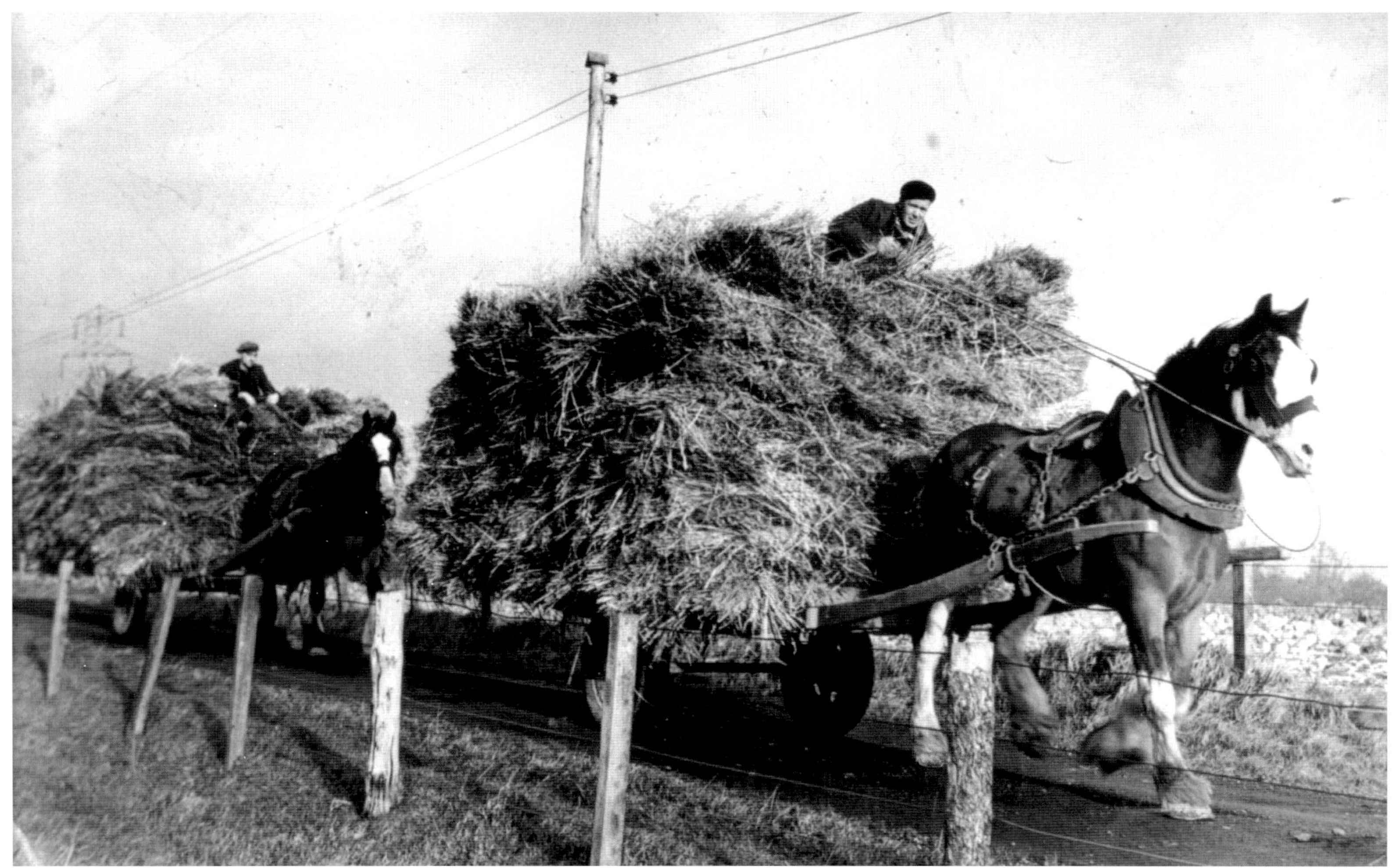

Clashbennie lies between Leetown and the river and this view shows the harvest being carted to the threshing mill from Mrs McDonald's pendicle (a small detached piece of a farm) at Chapelhill with her son Bill atop the second cart. Clashbennie Quarry, one of only two places within the bounds of the Carse where sandstone suitable for building was worked, should be known to all geologists, as it exercised a magnetic appeal to the pioneers, Hugh Miller and Louis Agassiz. They were astonished by the quantity and completeness of the fossil fish which they uncovered there.

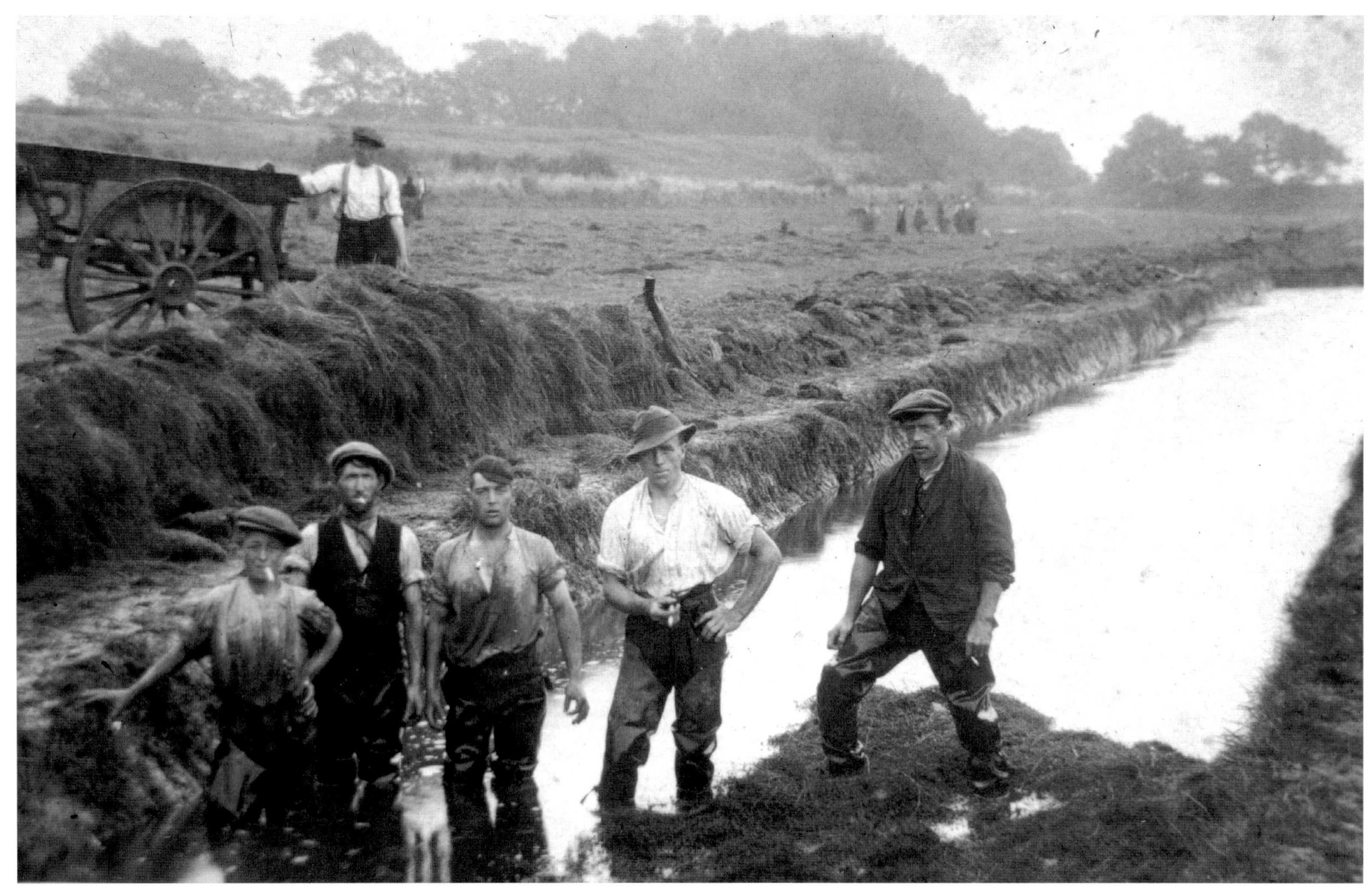

The subsoil conditions of Carse farms close to the river are well illustrated here, the necessity for good drainage to allow working of the fertile top soil being paramount. About 1921 workers at Nether Mains Farm between Glencarse and the river demonstrate how close to high water level some fields are. The alluvial soil has three distinct old 'sea-margins' at three, nine and fourteen feet respectively above the normal high water level of the River Tay.

          Nether Mains Farm

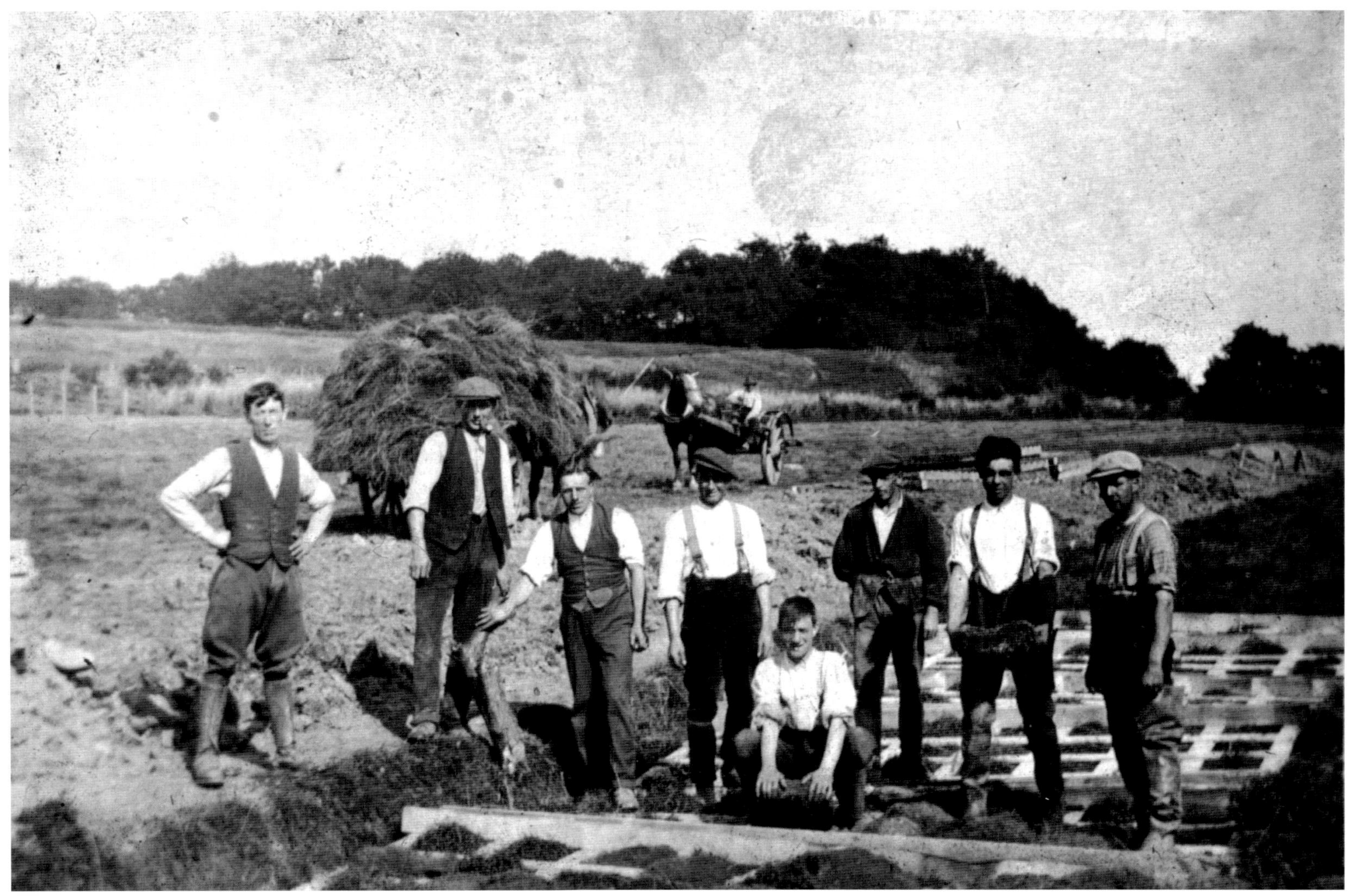

Farm workers at Nether Mains near Cairnie Pier also in 1921. It is possible that they are reinforcing the embankments which here retain flood water from the Tay. Clay from beside the river was used for such tasks, and also for brick making.

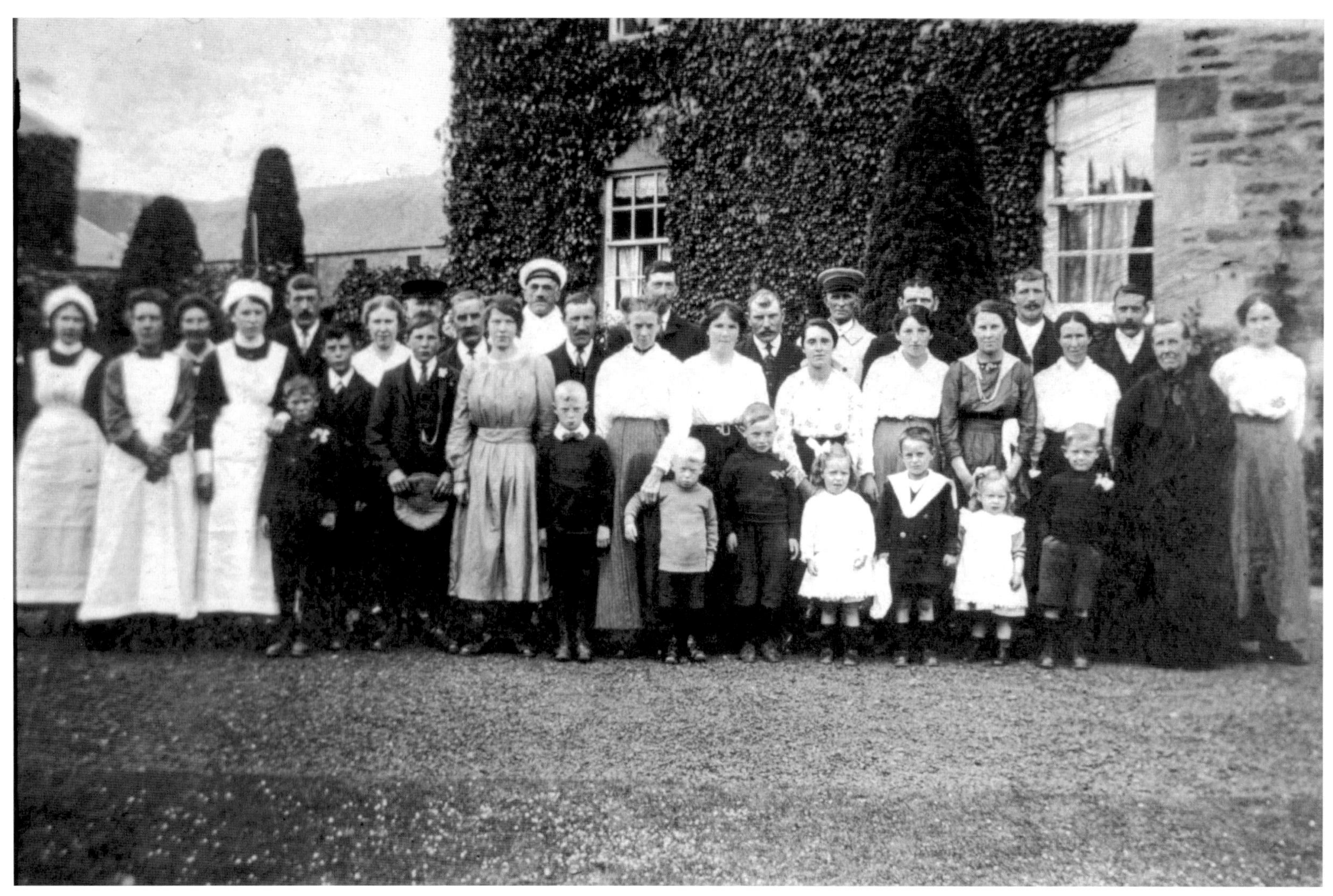

This photograph entitled 'Clashbennie with servants and maids' gives a very good indication of the numbers employed at the many large mansion houses of the Carse in days gone by. The wives of the farm hands would very often be employed as cooks or maids in the 'Big Hoose'.

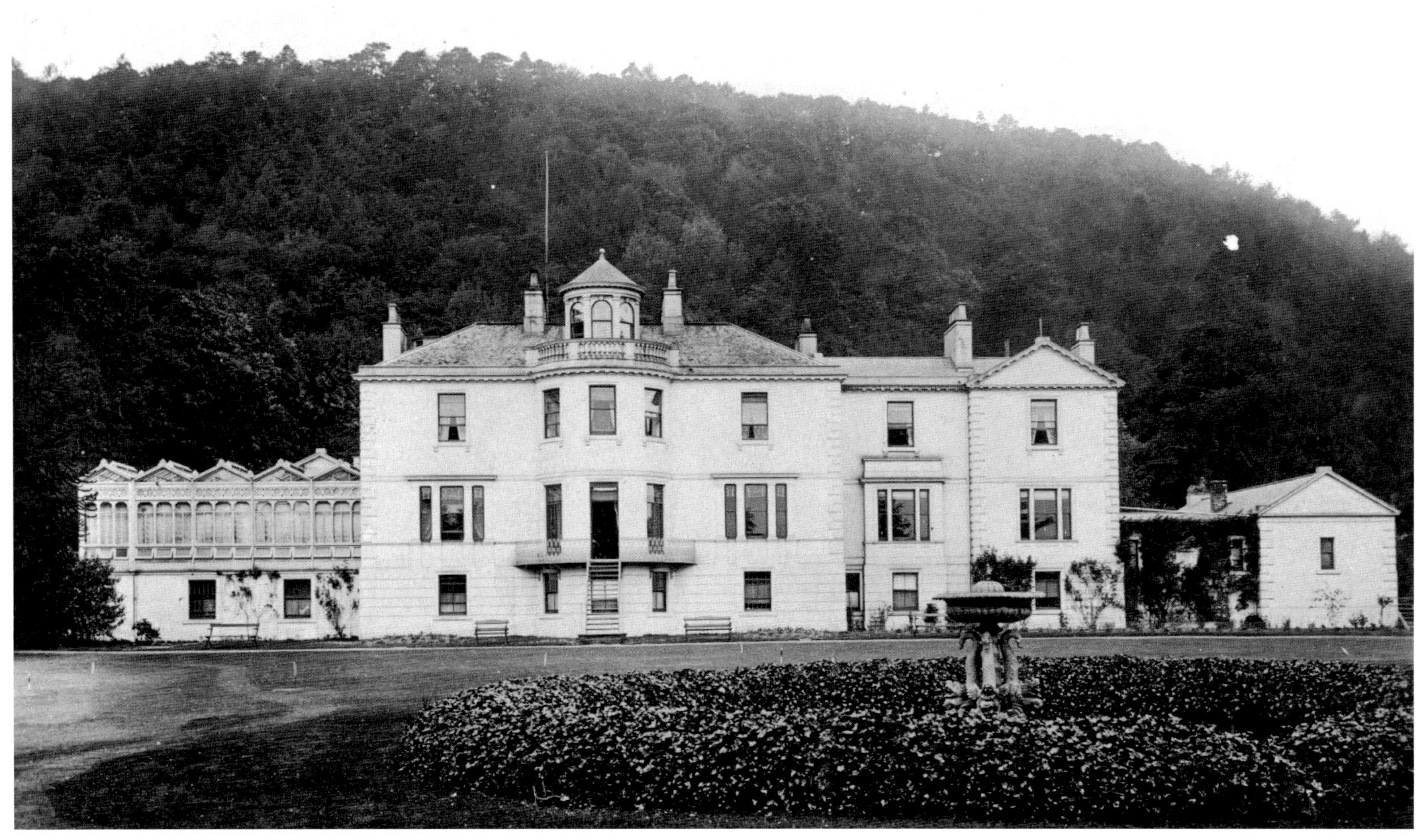

Glencarse House, photographed here in 1903, sits on higher ground above and behind the eponymous village. The mansion, a classical laird's house, was constructed in 1790 for Thomas Hunter, but has been comprehensively altered on several occasions since, not to its entire benefit, having been described authoritatively as 'a pompous mess'! The symetrical part surmounted by the highest cupola is original, but does not show its initial appearance.

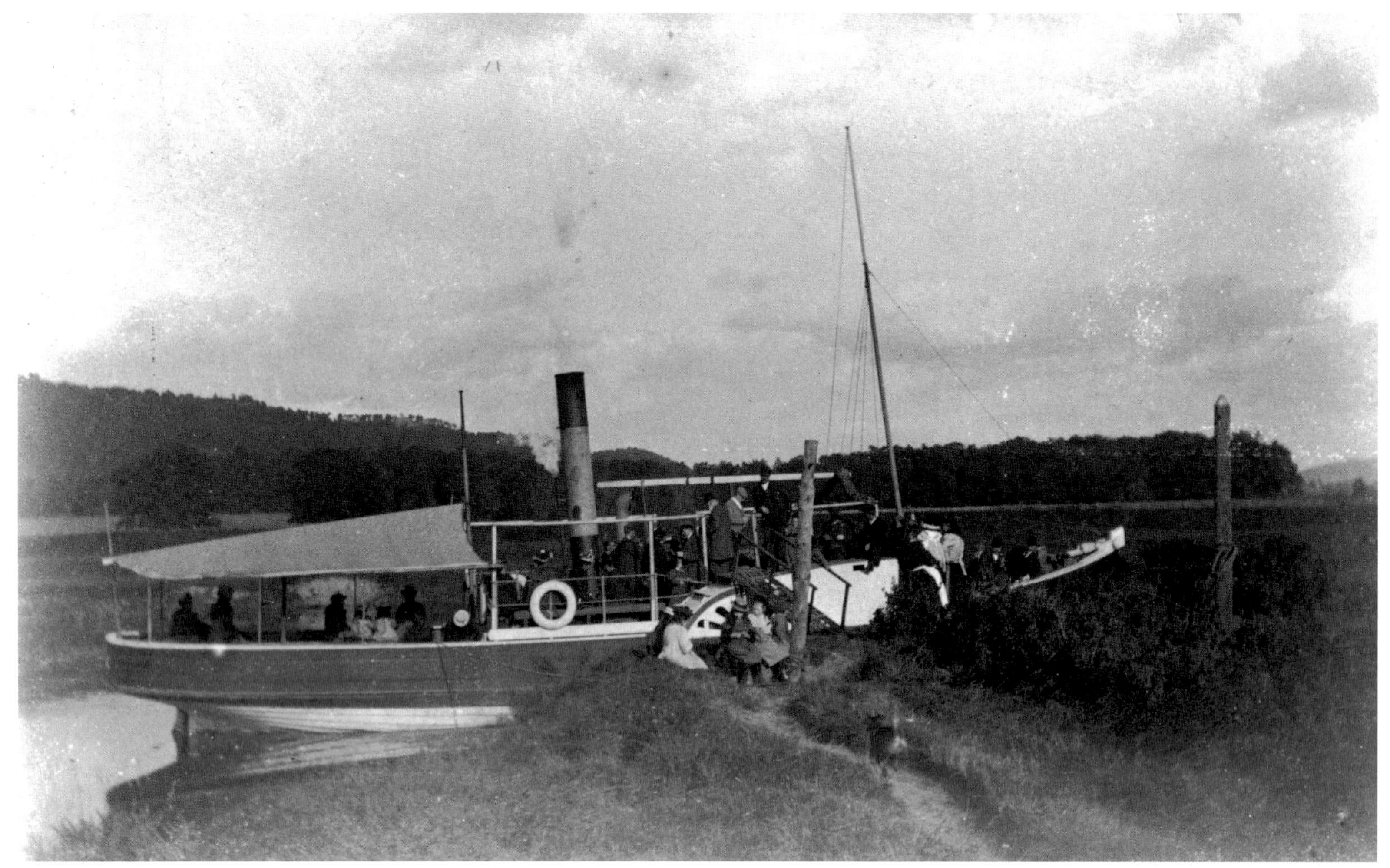

A trip up the Tay from Dundee in 1894 took the little steam tug *Queen* to Cairnie (or Cairney) Pier opposite the confluence of the Earn and the Tay. From Cairnie on the north side of the river a small ferry was intermittently available to cross over to Ferryfield of Carpow. The pier at Cairnie was improved by Sir John Richardson of Pitfour in the 1840s to allow access by steam ships, and two of these new-fangled devices, the *Lass of Gowrie* and the *Star of Gowrie* were put in service. The last boat used on the ferry, in the 1920s, is said to have been the *Emily Florence*.

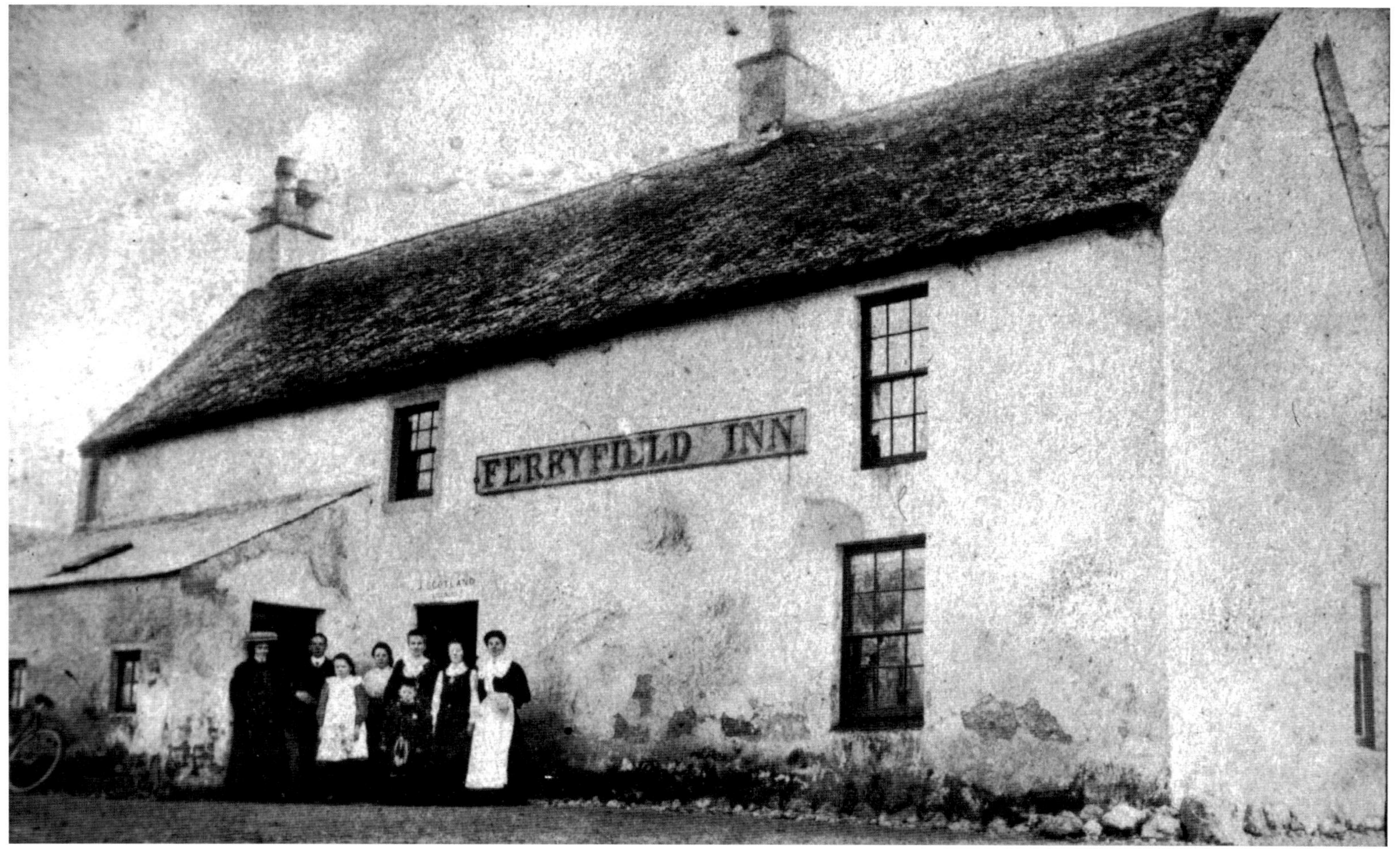

From Ferryfield of Carpow the ferry operated across the Tay to Cairnie, or over the Earn to Rhynd. These were important staging points on the old north to south drovers' roads. Inns were provided, both at Cairnie and as illustrated here, at Ferryfield, followed by another which has disappeared, the Duff Inn further south. The crossing here was known as the 'Loaf Ferry', a legend recounting how MacDuff, fleeing south after the murder of Macbeth, and having not a penny on him for the fare, paid the ferryman with a loaf of bread. In early years the crossing was known as 'Aitken's Boat'. The old Inn at Ferryfield seen here has since been transformed into a dwelling house.

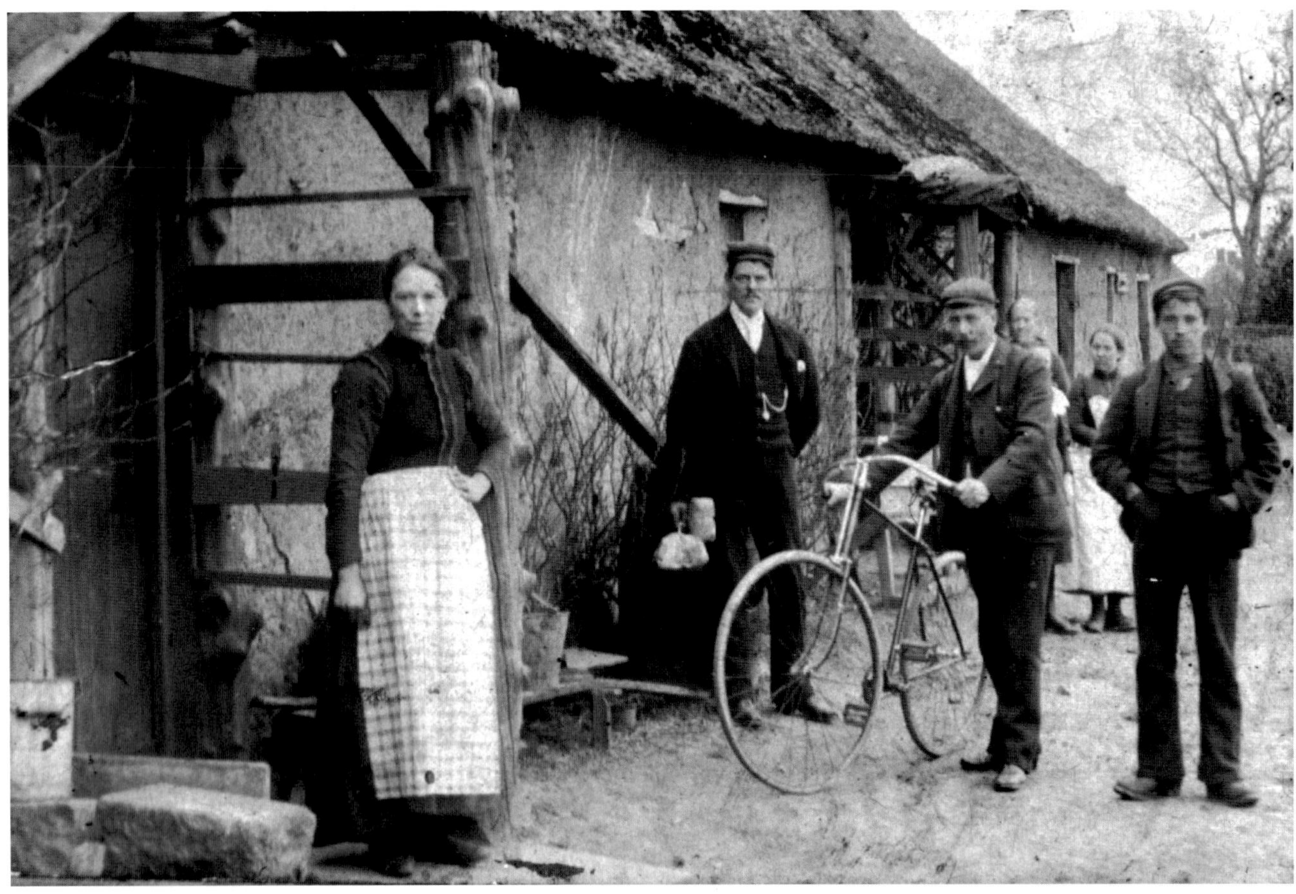

Leetown and its neighbour Cottown grew up as agricultural workers' settlements. With building stone difficult to find in the Carse, it was a case two hundred years ago of 'every man his own mason', and many workers' houses were built with clay walls (the clay dug locally, reinforced with straw then lime-wash coated) and thatched (thackit) roofs, the thatch being reeds from the river's edge. These hand-crafted dwellings could achieve surprising longevity when well maintained and one such example, the Old Schoolhouse in Cottown, is approaching completion of its restoration. Reed thatching with local materials was undertaken until in 1991 the final specialist company involved (Reedways) was hit by the regional assessor for business rates for this naturally growing product. Although worked thereafter by Tayreed, imported cheaper material from Europe finally forced closure in April 2005. Earlier that year, a lease of some 100 hectares of the reed bed was taken up by the RSPB, to be managed for the good of the bird population. The Carse is unique, with 15% of the entire reed beds of the United Kingdom found along the banks of the River Tay.

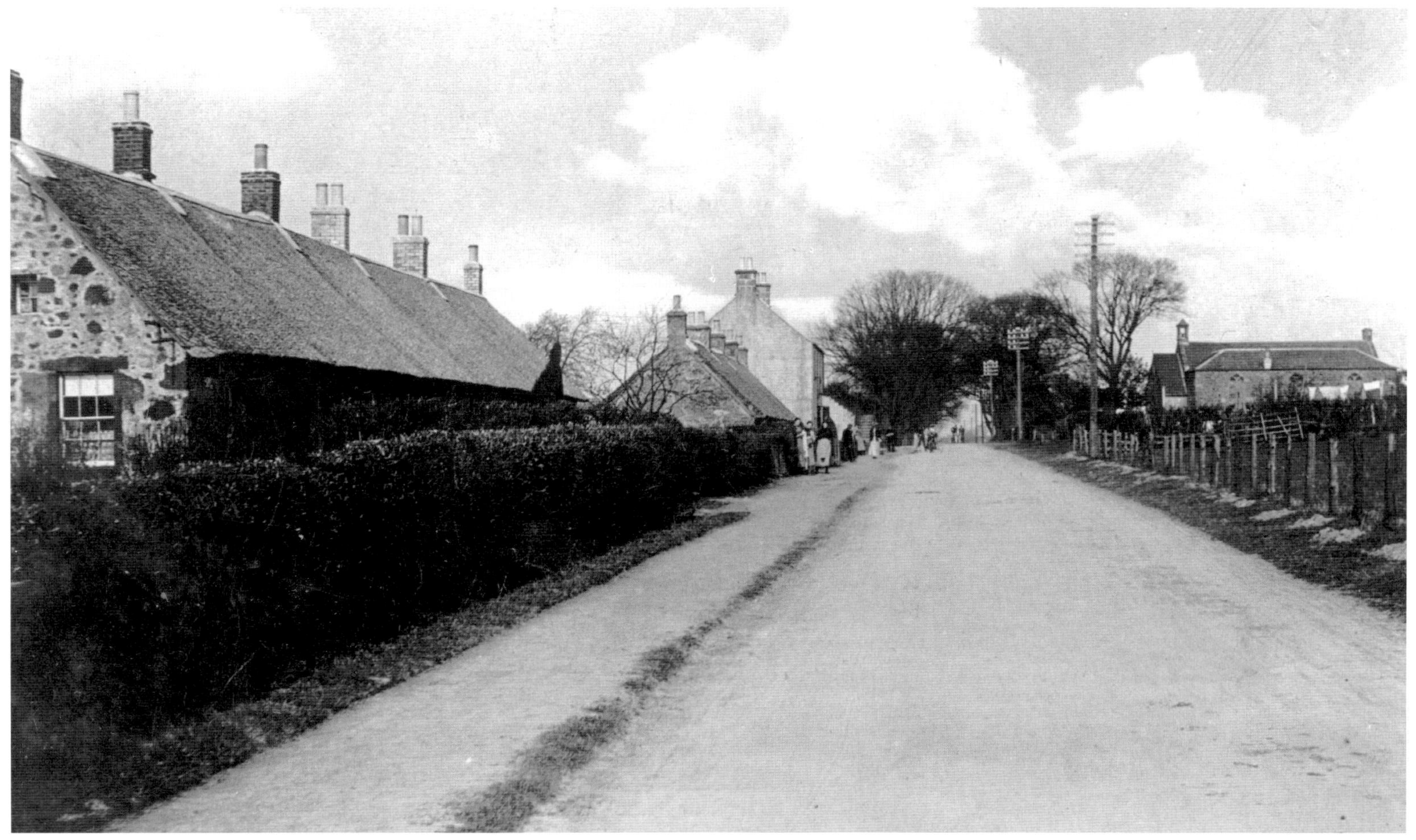

Just a mile east along the Dundee road from Glencarse, the next former agricultural settlement is Glendoick, now perhaps best known for its popular garden centre. Another mansion house, Glendoick House of circa 1747 and possibly designed by William Adam, sits north of the estate hamlet, built for Lord Craigie, Lord President of the Court of Session and has been described as 'one of the loveliest examples of early Georgian architecture in Scotland'. The cottages on the left of the picture will be thatched with reeds from the local beds in the Tay. The greatly widened main road has irreversibly altered the nature and look of the village of which no vestige of the houses shown here remain. Apart from the primary school, one of the few remaining original buildings is a lodge of Glendoick House.

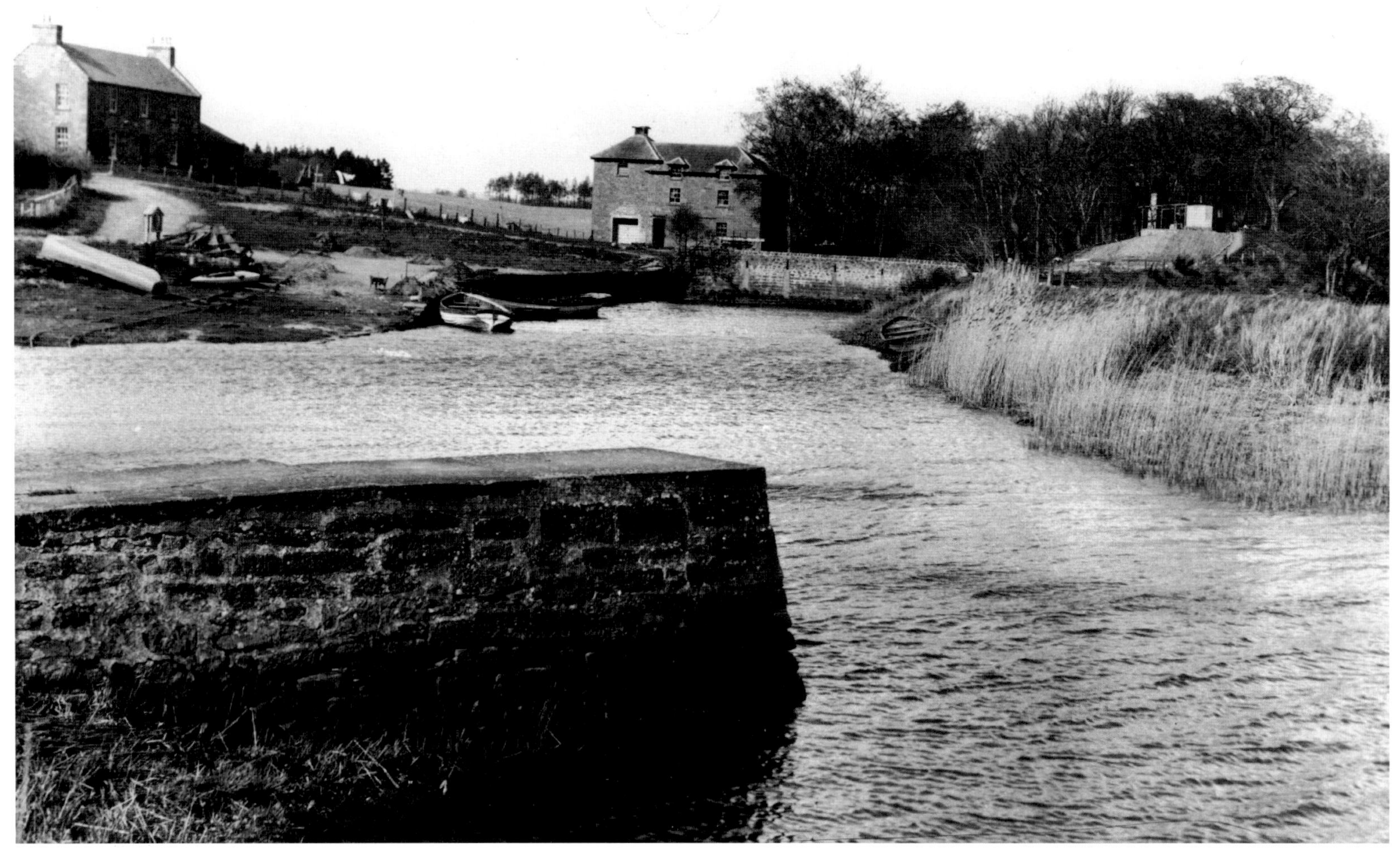

For many busy years prior to construction of the railway Port Allen served as the main point for trade into and out of the west Carse around Errol. In an average year the busy little port could see the import of over 1,000 tons of coal and 5,000 bolls of agricultural lime. At one time the tiny harbour supported a population of over 50 souls and had an inn, a meal mill and a toll house. The old mill, beyond the bridge has now disappeared completely. Here a chain across the road formerly prevented anybody avoiding payment for the use of the pier. The pillars remain – without the chain – but they have been moved from their original positions. The reed beds here now are a paradise for bird-watchers.

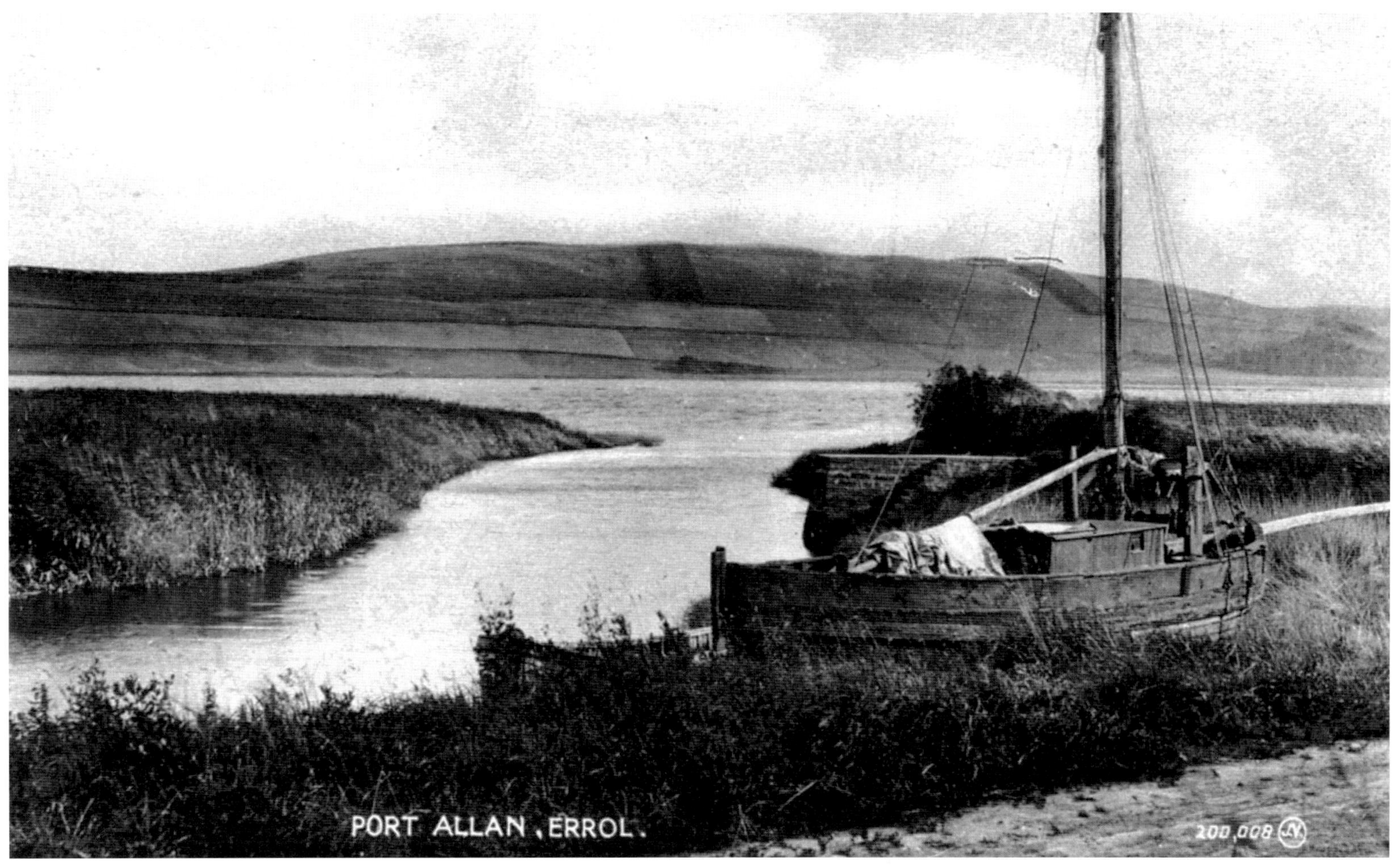

Port Allen (not 'Allan' as wrongly inscribed on this card, as it was definitely named for John Lee Allen, who implemented many land improvements – previously it had been known as Pow of Errol) had had its day a hundred years before this photo was taken in 1926. At one time a daily 'passage-boat' plied to and from Newburgh (by John Brown 'Boat Jack') at a cost of 6d per trip. In the 1930s a boat here became a home to George 'Skipper' Davidson who salted eels caught in the river. George lived in a bothy at that time and later lived in the saloon of an old Dundee tramcar. It was said that he had one of the ship's lifeboats from the Mauretania for salmon fishing!

The large farm of Mains of Errol lies just to the west of the village of the same name and inland on the road to Port Allen. The changed nature of farming is illustrated in these scenes of life on the farm less than a hundred years ago. (A) Before mechanisation the farm stud amounted to eight 'horse-power', and until recently use of such magnificent beasts was demonstrated at the Heavy Horse Centre at Newton Farm by Walnut Grove. (B) Alex Downie ploughing at Mains of Errol. (C) Chic Downie with the first Fordson tractor at Mains of Errol; it has been said that at one time 70% of tractors in the world were Fordsons. (D) Will Somerville cutting river reeds for thatching.

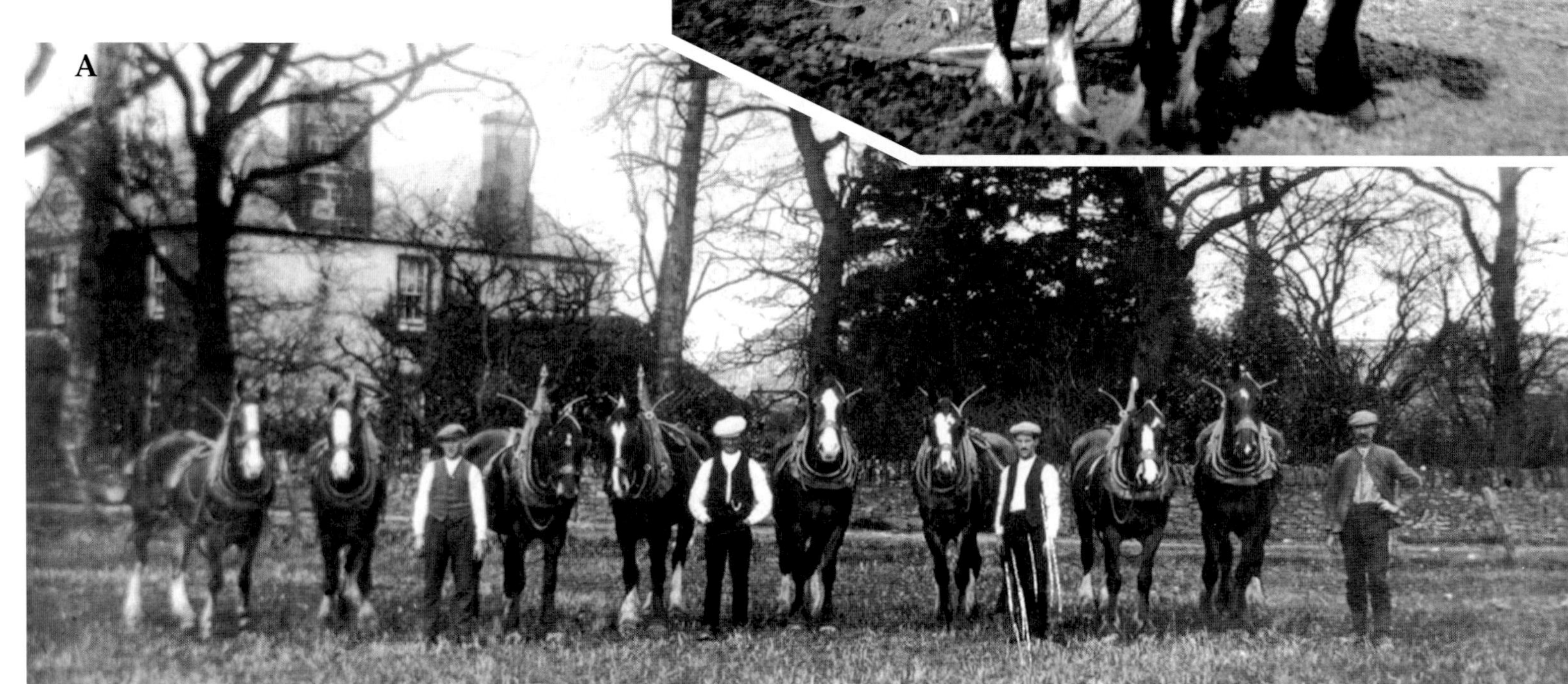

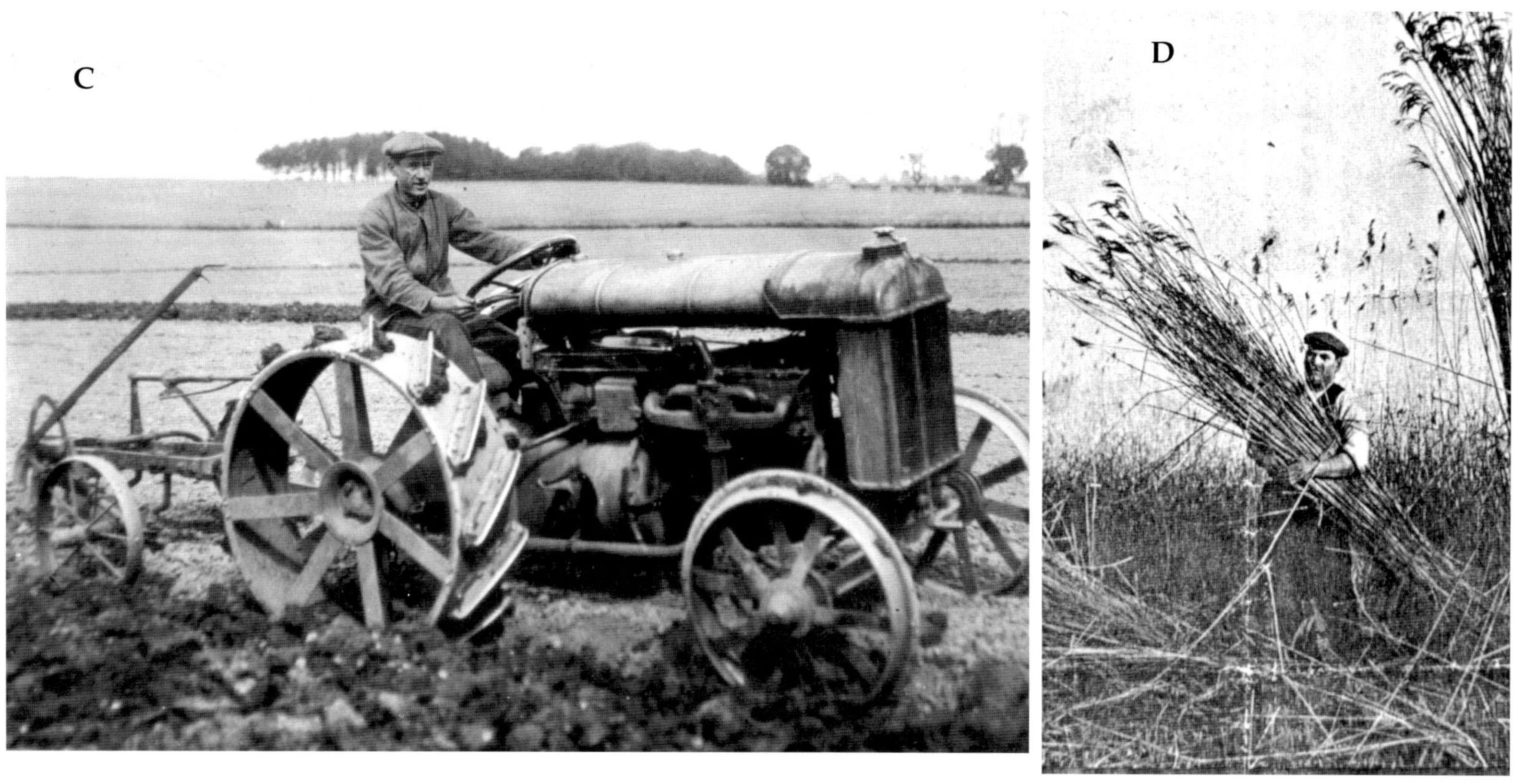
C
D

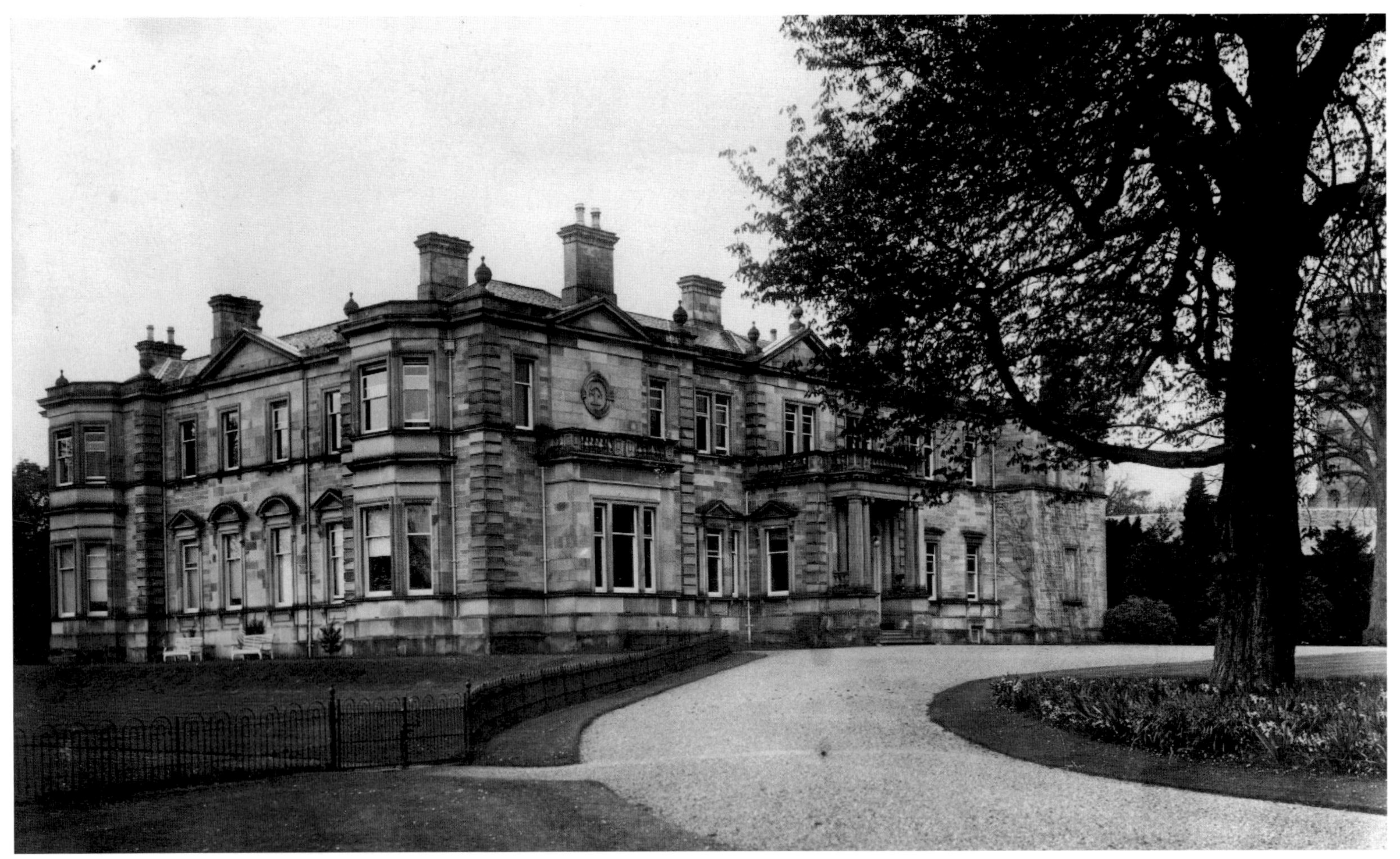

The 'B' listed Errol Park sits west of the village and was built in 1875-1877, immediately following destruction by fire of its predecessor which stood on the same site. Of a style described as nineteenth century Renaissance, it was utilised by a French television company as an appropriate setting for their filming of Pierre Choderlos de Laclos' 'Les Liaisons Dangereuses'. The earlier house had been the seat of Captain John Lee Allen RN who added over 100 acres to the estate by building the eleven foot high embankments along the river's edge to restrain the frequent inundation of the low fields by flooding. The park around the house is noted as being of national significance, and contains, along with stunning specimen trees, an unusual oval bowling green.

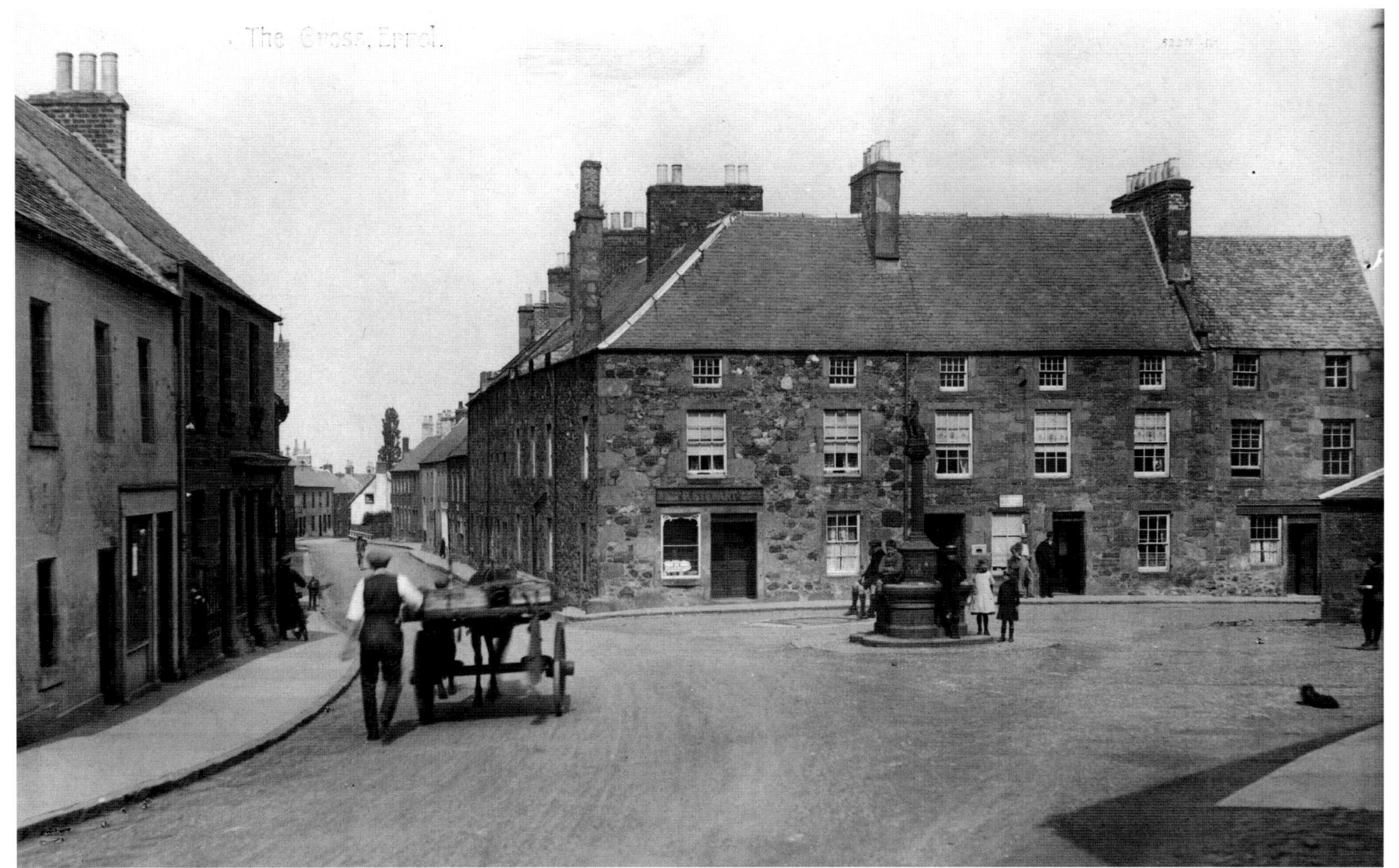

This 1919 view looks east at Errol Cross. Many of the old houses are built in red sandstone from Clashbennie Quarry, but there are also many examples, unusually for rural Scotland, of brick buildings and older cottages with walls of Carse clay. A brick and tile works was built, also at the instigation of John Lee Allen, to promote agricultural field drainage and build agricultural workers' cottages. Occupying the central spot is, not a market cross, but a long dried up fountain, erected by the proprietor of Errol Park to commemorate the Diamond Jubilee of Queen Victoria, carrying the inscription '1837 VR 1897'.

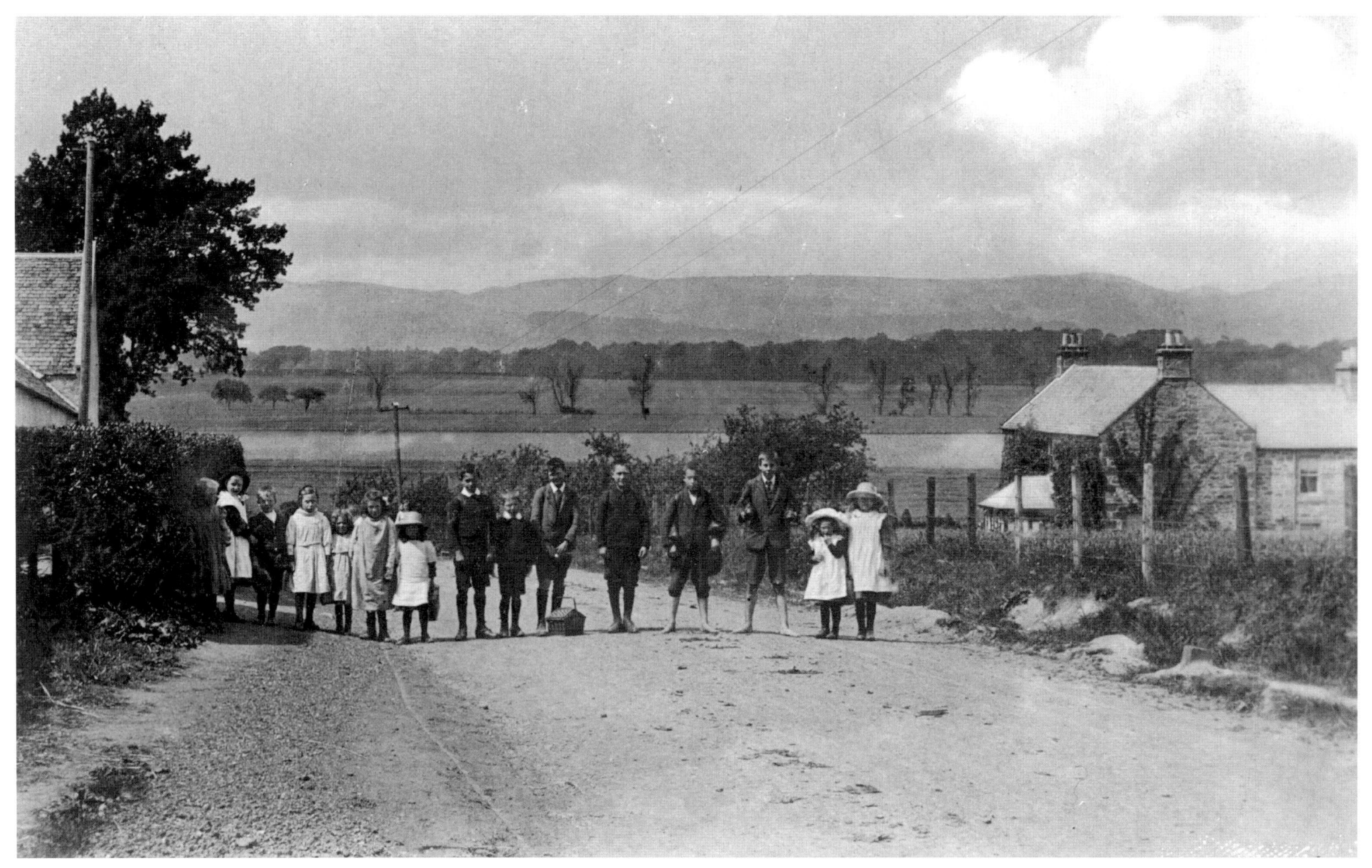

Errol village stands elevated above the Carse lands, an obvious location for a settlement above potential inundation from flooding. In earlier times the village was a centre for handloom weaving of coarse linen and canvas. This postcard view, published by Lundie of Dundee, of Errol Loan from Woodlands Lodge looking north across the unchanged vista of the Carse to the Sidlaw Hills behind, has ensured good sales by recording more than a dozen of the local children.

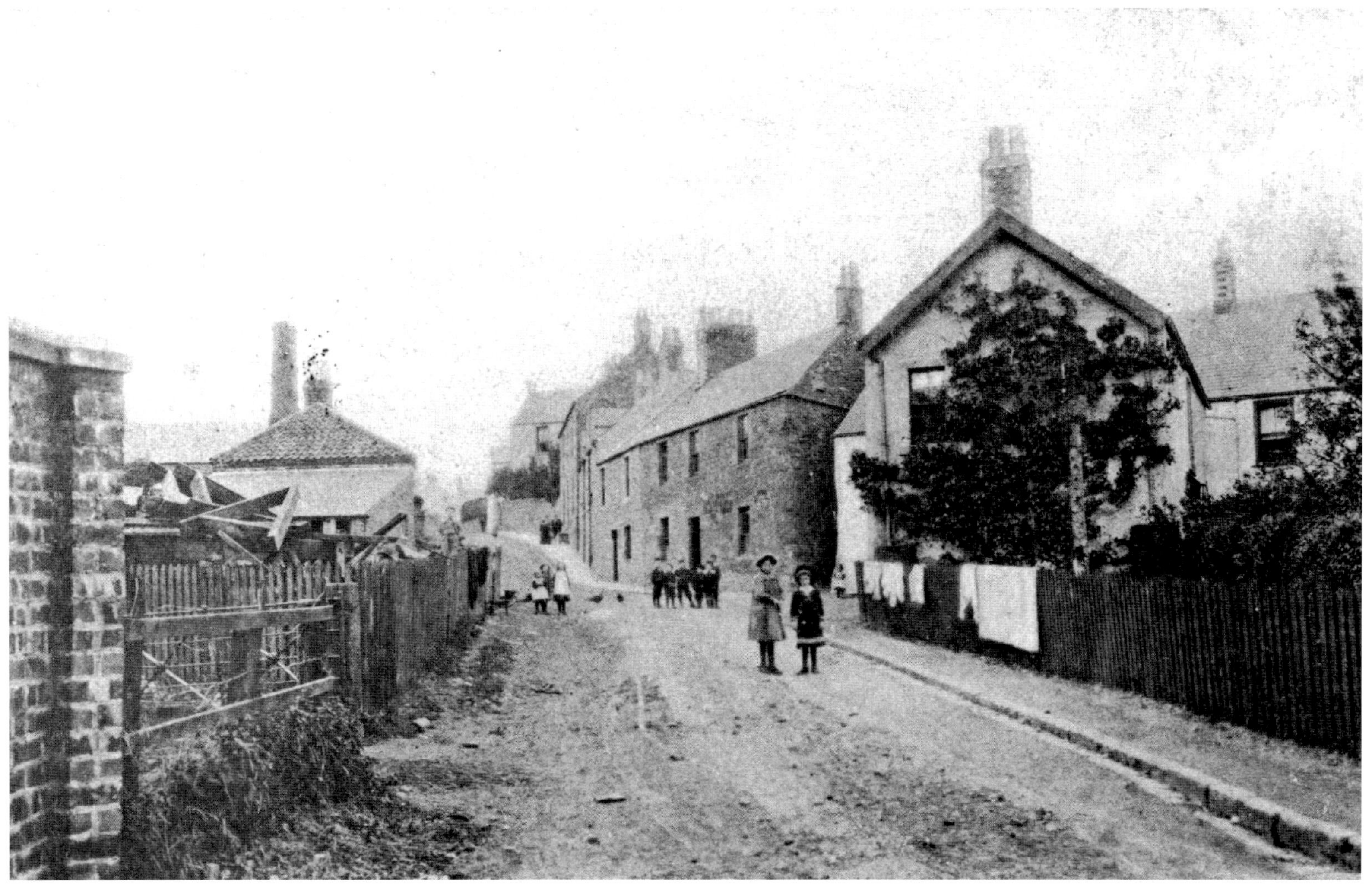

Gas Work Brae led south to the small gas works on the left of the scene which supplied the villagers' needs for many years from 1850. Electricity arrived in 1933. The lane was known as Kiln Brae before construction of the gas works, perhaps indicating the existence of an earlier industrial use of the site. It is now just 'Gas Brae'.

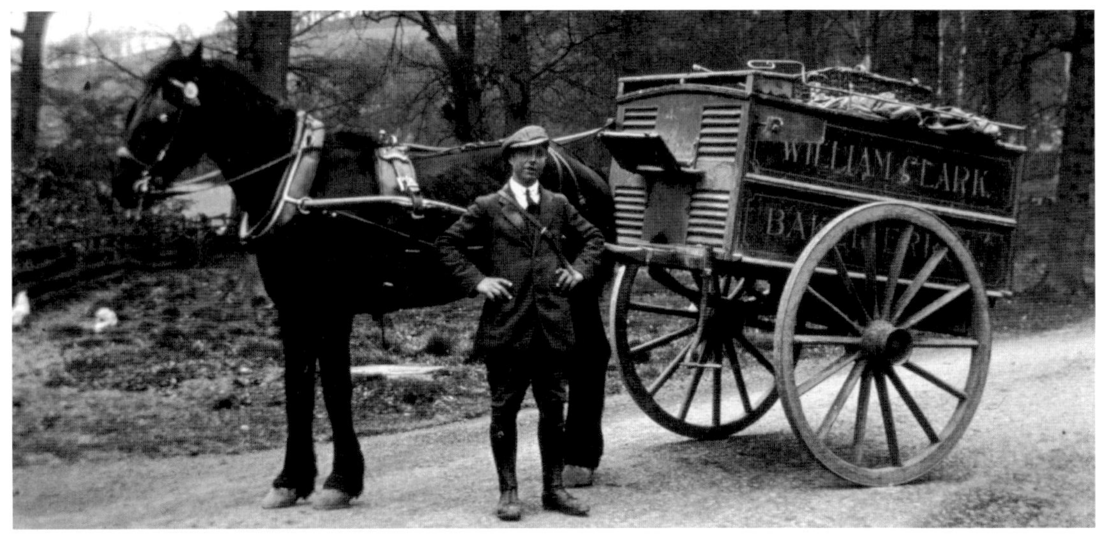
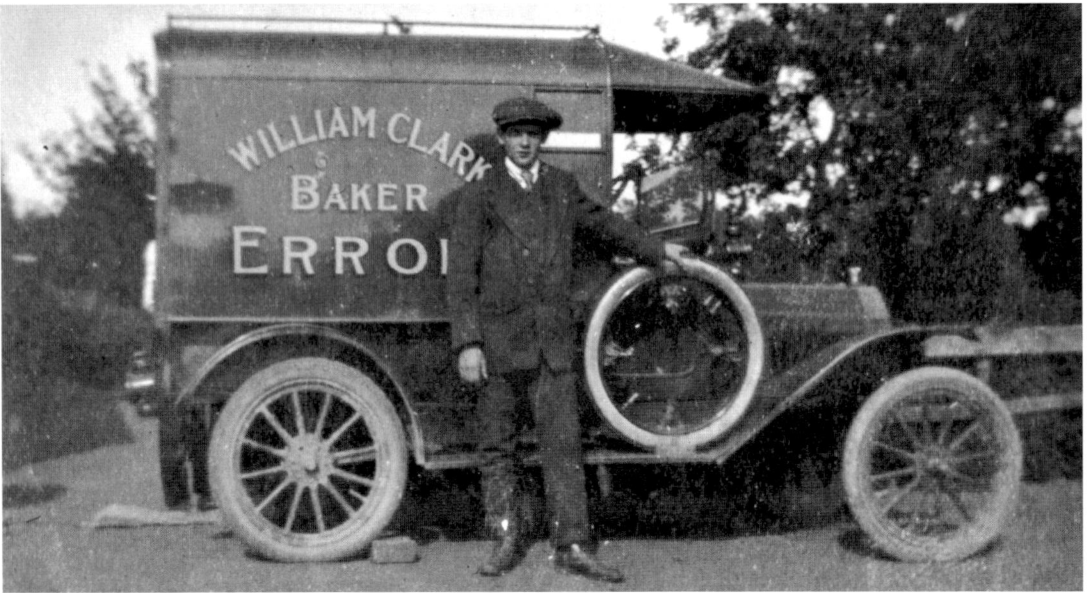

Alex Bruce who worked for William Clark, baker in Errol, with the spring cart used to make deliveries to the nearer farms and settlements until a motor van replaced.

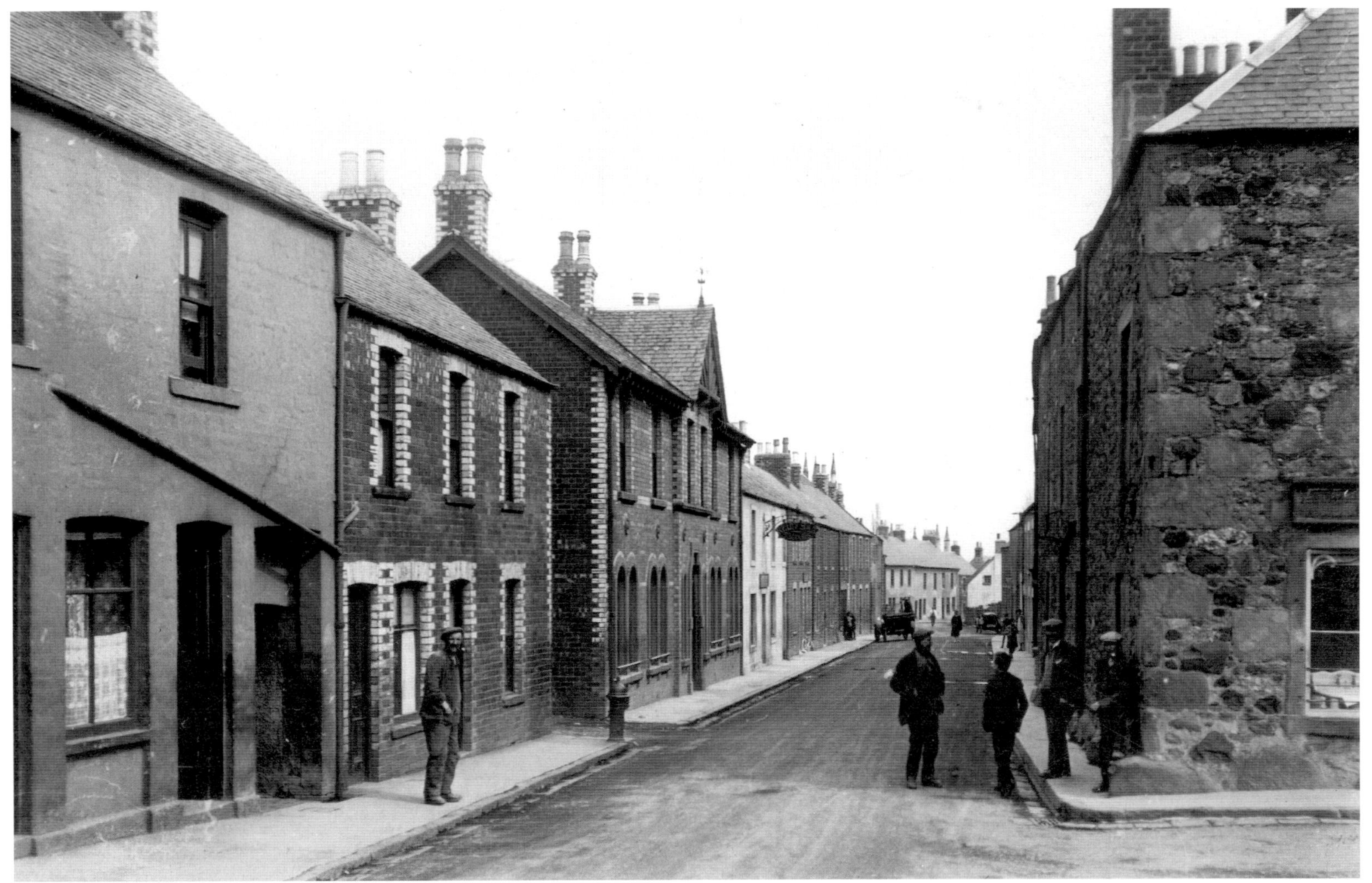

On the north side of this view of Errol High Street can be seen several of the buildings constructed using the output of Inchcoonans brickworks. Inchcoonans bricks are said to have been used in construction of both the first and second Tay railway bridges at Dundee. This long-established major local employer has closed recently after over 150 years continuous use.

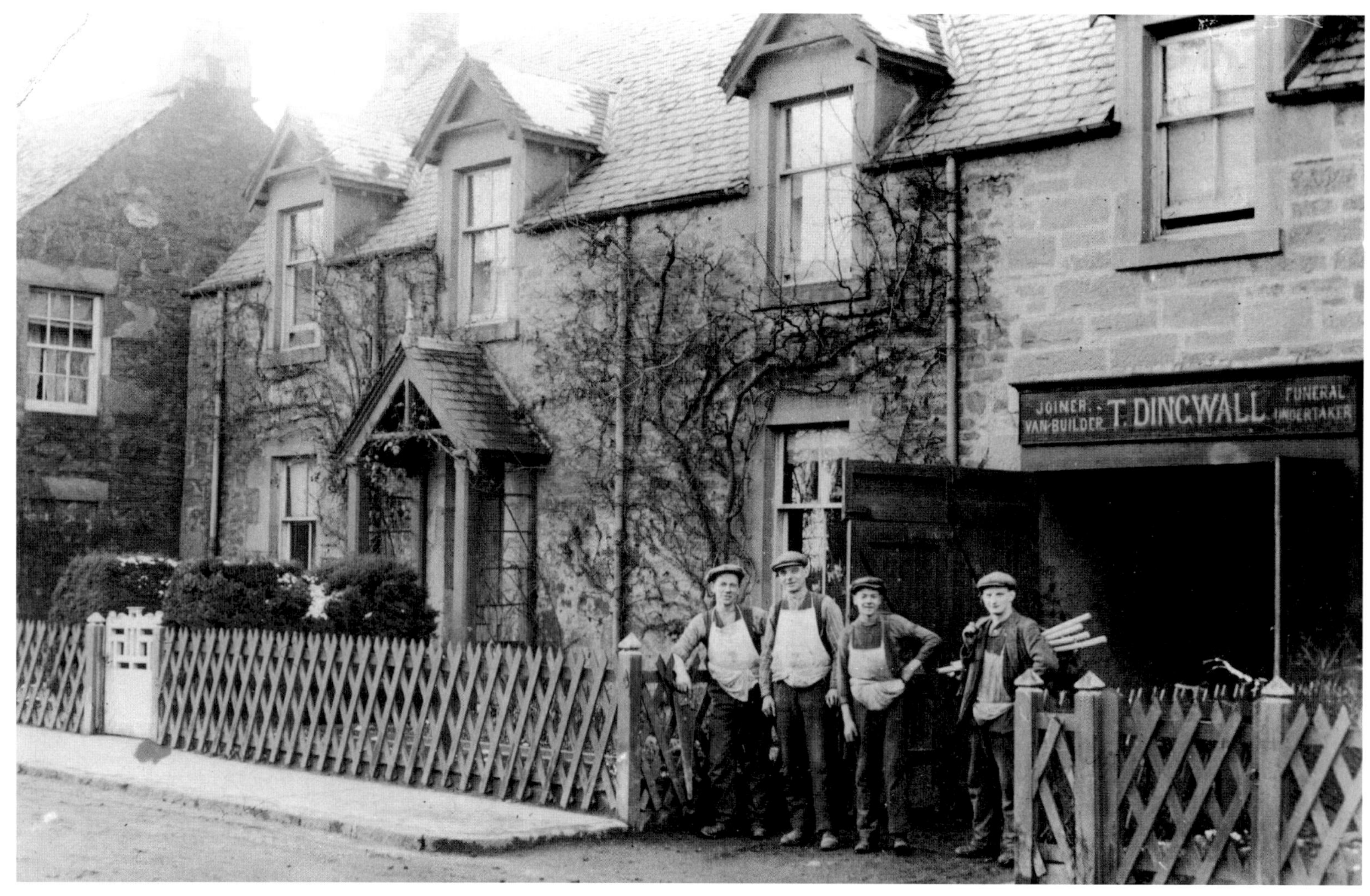

Joinery and undertaking were two professions which went together in small communities. Dingwall's business was at the west end of Errol High Street, and seen in this 1920s scene are, left to right Ken Sinclair, George Sorrie, William Logie and Bill Strachan.

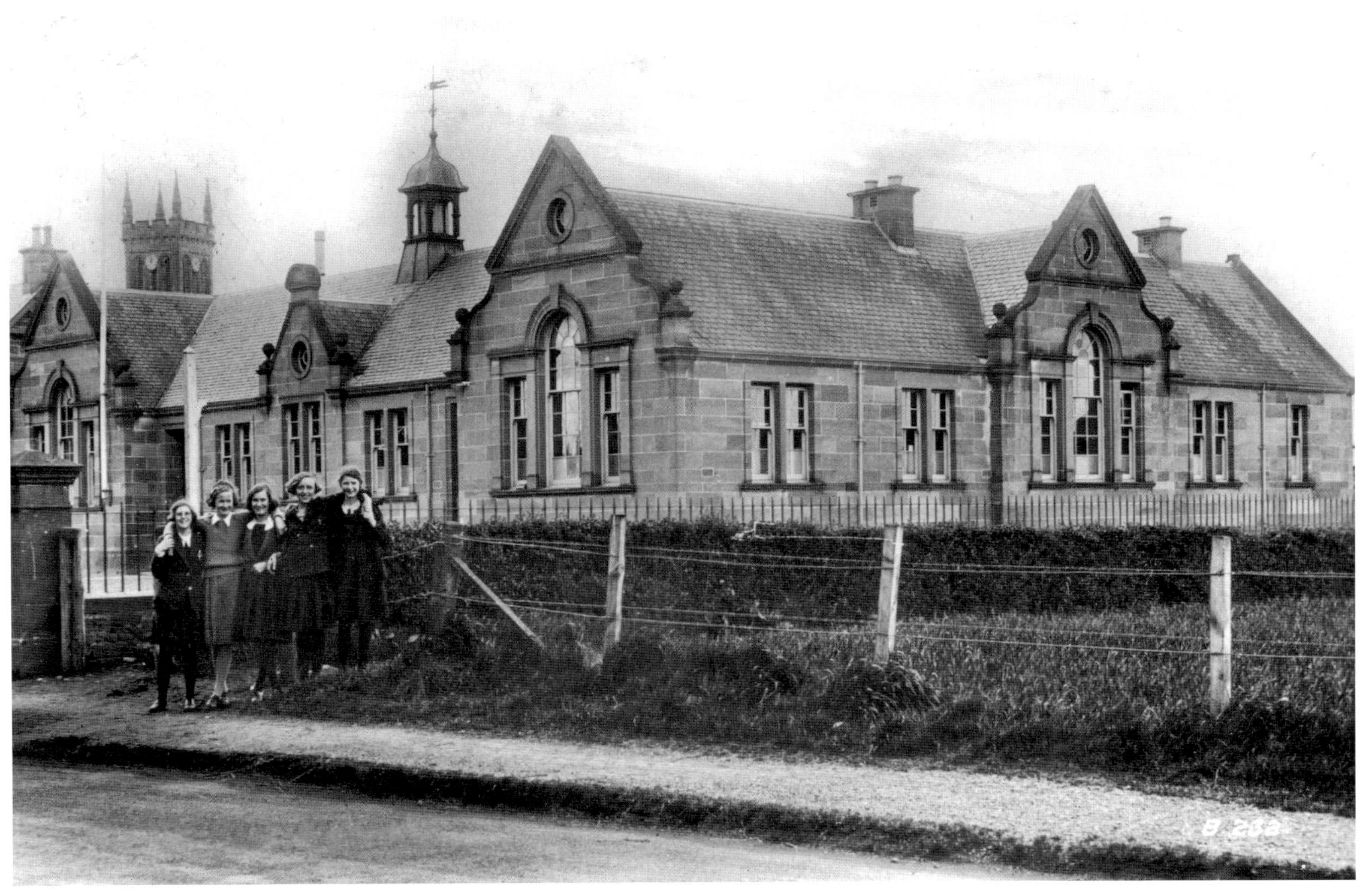

Five bonnie Errol lassies at the Public School in School Wynd. The sender of this old card 'Alice' has written "… do you know any one on the picture?" Presumably she is one of the five. Can anybody identify the others in this scene from over seventy years ago? The handsome structure dated from the 1860s, and has been given a new lease of life as housing. On the left, above the roof can just be seen the top of the tower of the parish church.

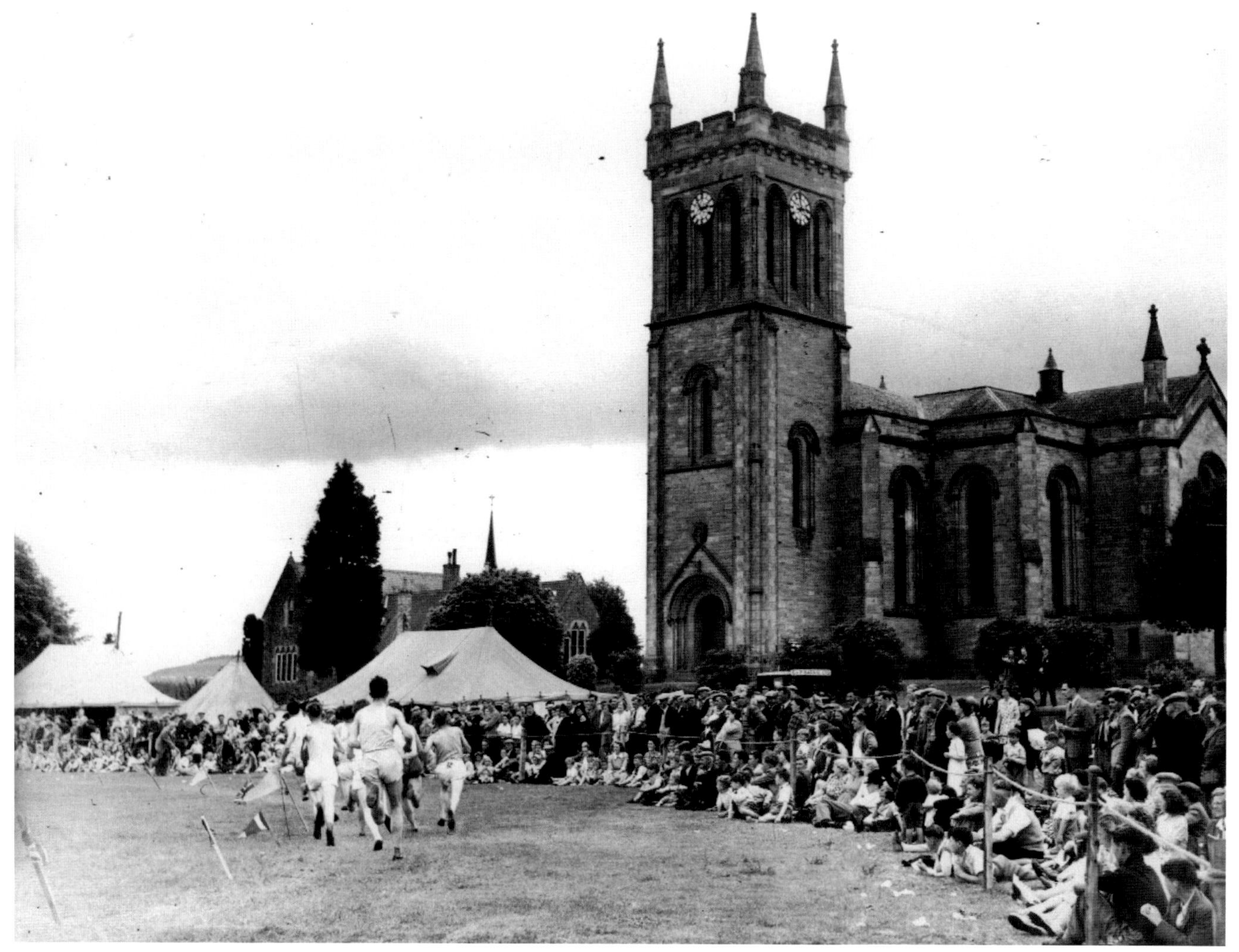

Boys' race at Errol Races on The Green in the early sixties. Overlooking the scene is the bulk of the parish church, fondly known as 'The Cathedral of the Carse'. The church opened in March 1833, having been constructed for a cost of £3,819. Errol Races in former years were a magnet drawing visitors from afar, but these were horse races on the public road down to Inchcoonans gates and back which ceased at the time of the First World War.

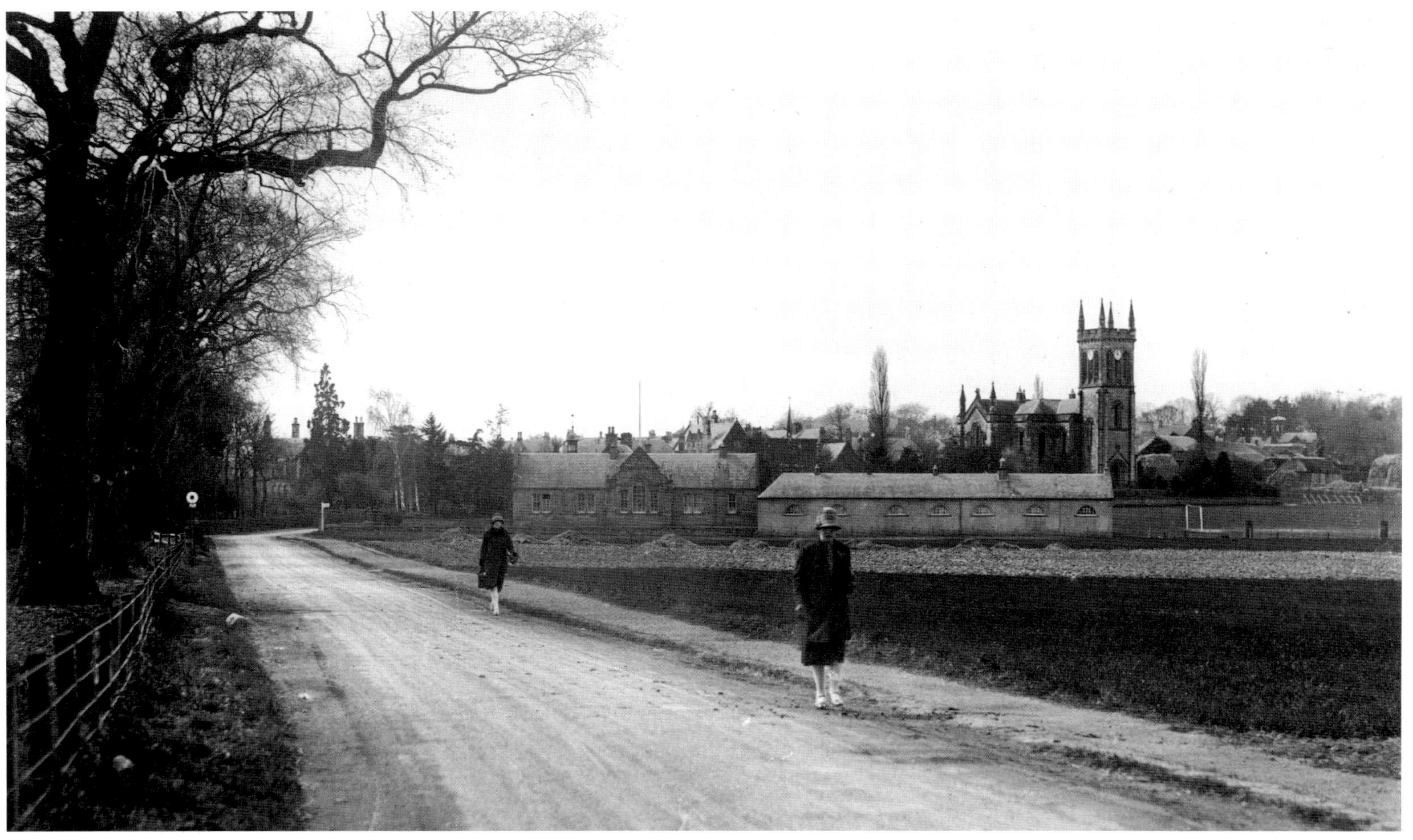

A general view of Errol some seventy years ago from Station Road. Errol village was more than a mile from its station and at one stage a horse (later a motor) bus ran between the two. Near here Preston Watson, Scotland's pioneer aviator, tried his first flying machine – an ornithopter – or flapping wing type aircraft. He later built two more conventionally powered machines and at one time was thought to have pre-dated the first powered flight made by the Wright Brothers in America, but he himself never claimed this achievement. The area to the right is now under development for yet more private housing, with more of the Carse lands giving way to the seeming inexhaustible demand for anodyne housing.

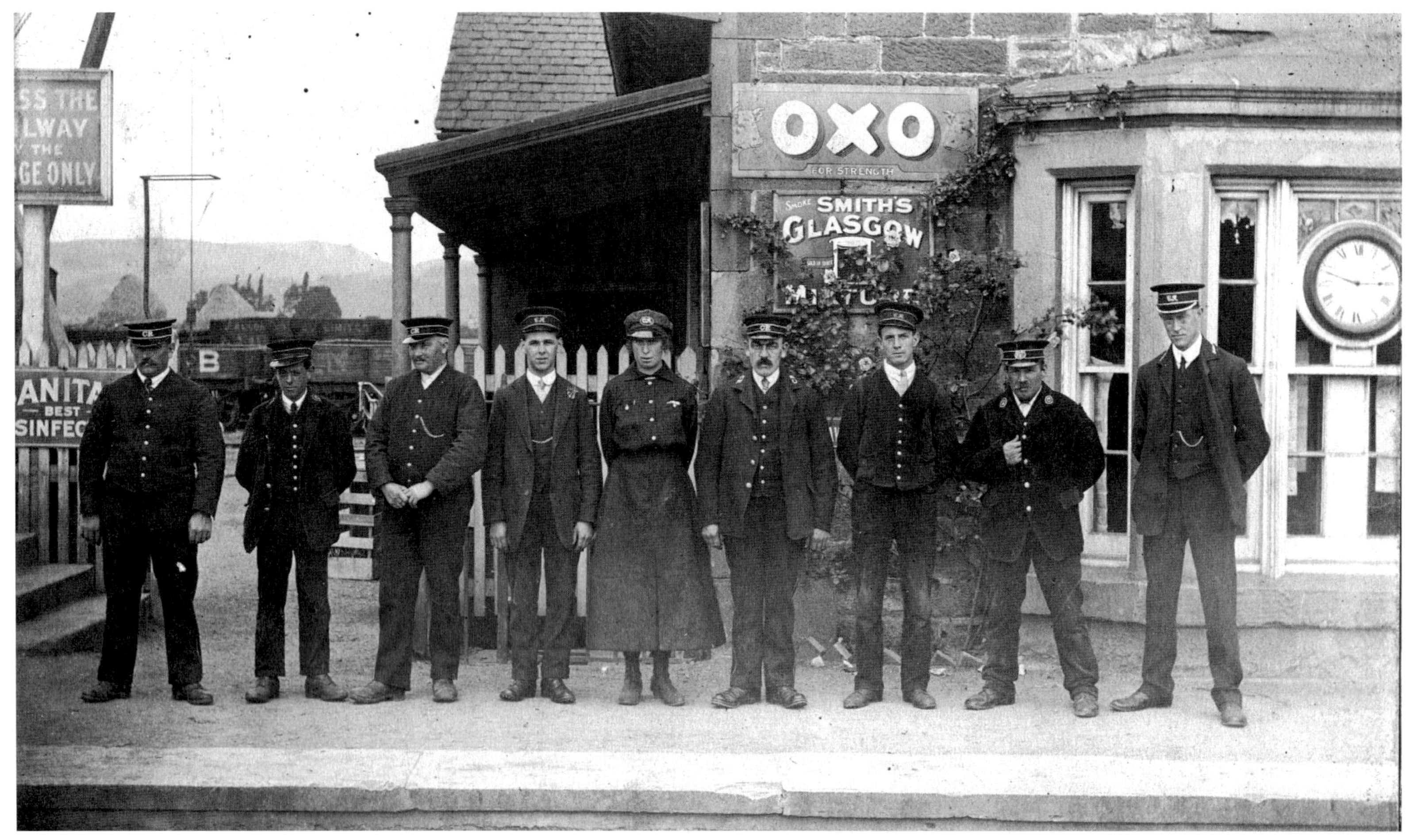

Errol Station staff photographed in February 1918. From left to right; Tom Calder (signalman), Andrew Duff (lamp boy), Bob Douglas (signalman), Alex Reid (clerk), Agnes Robertson (lady porter), Archie Rattray (signalman), Jim Cooper (booking clerk), Sandy Bell (porter), John Cameron (stationmaster); a remarkable number of people to operate a relatively small station. Cameron left the area in 1923 and became Superintendent at Lothian Road Goods Station, Edinburgh, eventually retiring in 1942. Errol Station building was constructed in 1847 (the date is on the gable above the station clock) and was closed on 28 September 1985. A 14 seat 'Reo' bus (ES7869) was, at one time, run to and from the village by David McIntosh, at the seemingly exorbitant fare of 4d! [Photo courtesy Lindsay Horne]

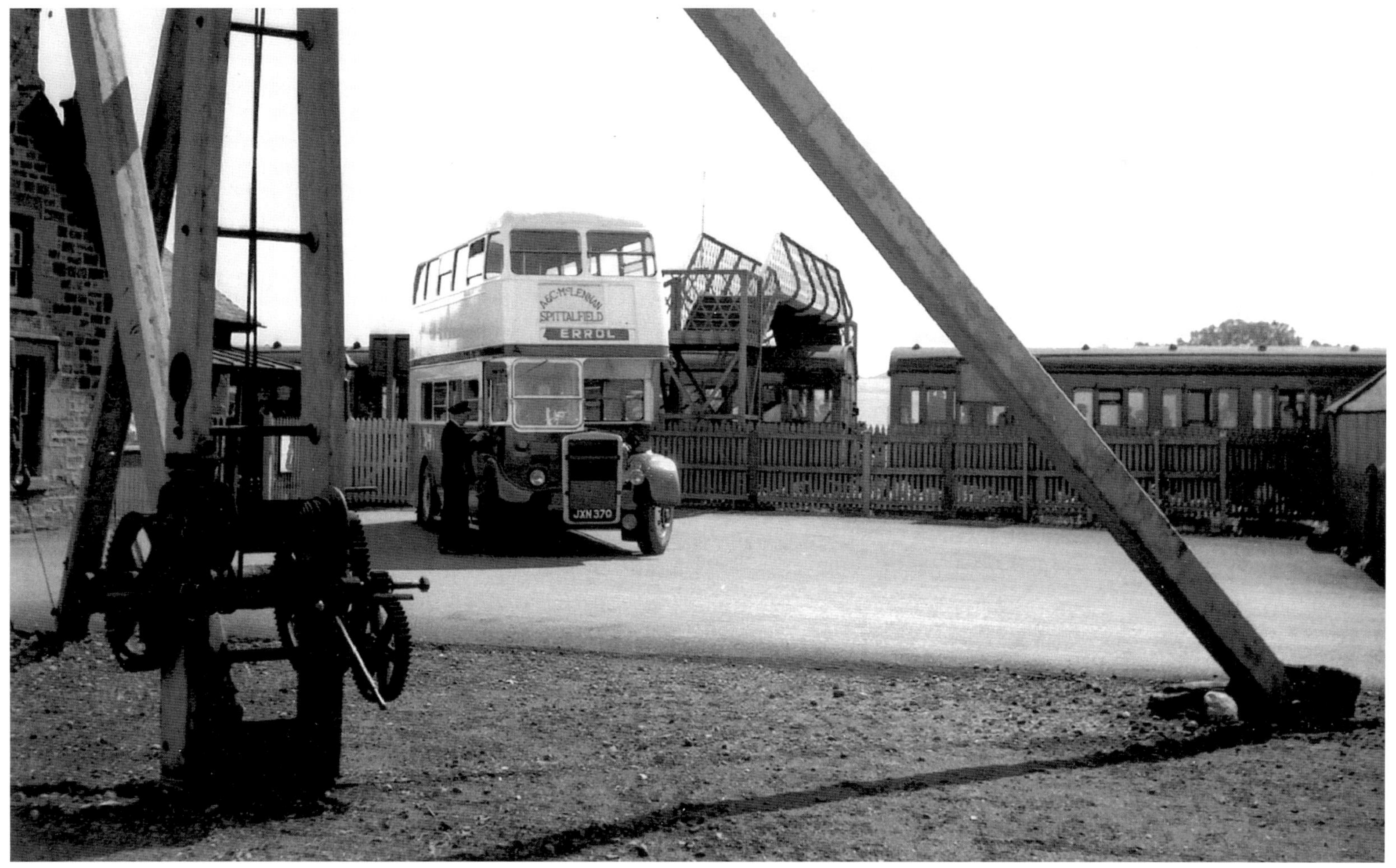

Errol Station yard was the terminus of two services operated by A & C McLellan of Spittalfield, one east to Dundee, the other west to Perth. Here in the station yard, framed by a hand operated crane, is McLellan's 1949 built former London Transport Leyland JXN370 (RTL47), purchased second-hand in 1958. McLellan's dark blue and white vehicles were always turned out in immaculate condition. After closure, Errol Station was preserved as a railway museum by volunteers between 1990 and 1999, but even this has now closed. [Photo courtesy Ian Maclean]

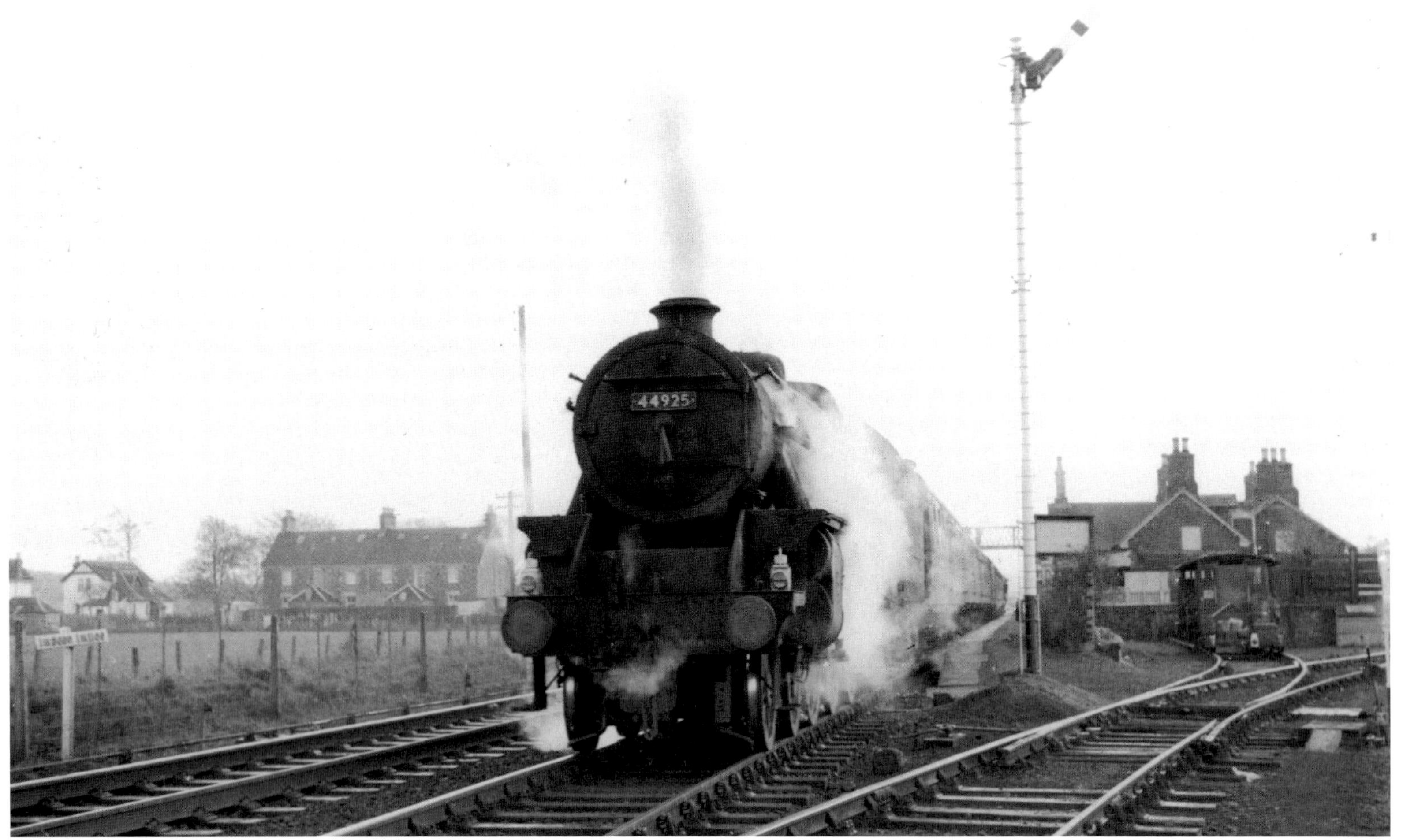

At Errol Station on 24 April 1965, Class '5' locomotive number 44925 is hauling the 06.15 from Glasgow to Dundee (West). In the former goods yard to the right to this day the platform edge is formed from ancient stone railway sleeper blocks which date from the time of the earliest railways in Scotland. It was planned, when the railway was built, to construct a branch to North Lodge on the Rait Road. Some work was carried out but the line was never completed. A deep cutting, just north of the station, which now takes the road past South and East Inchmichael provides a lasting reminder of this. [Courtesy Hamish Stevenson]

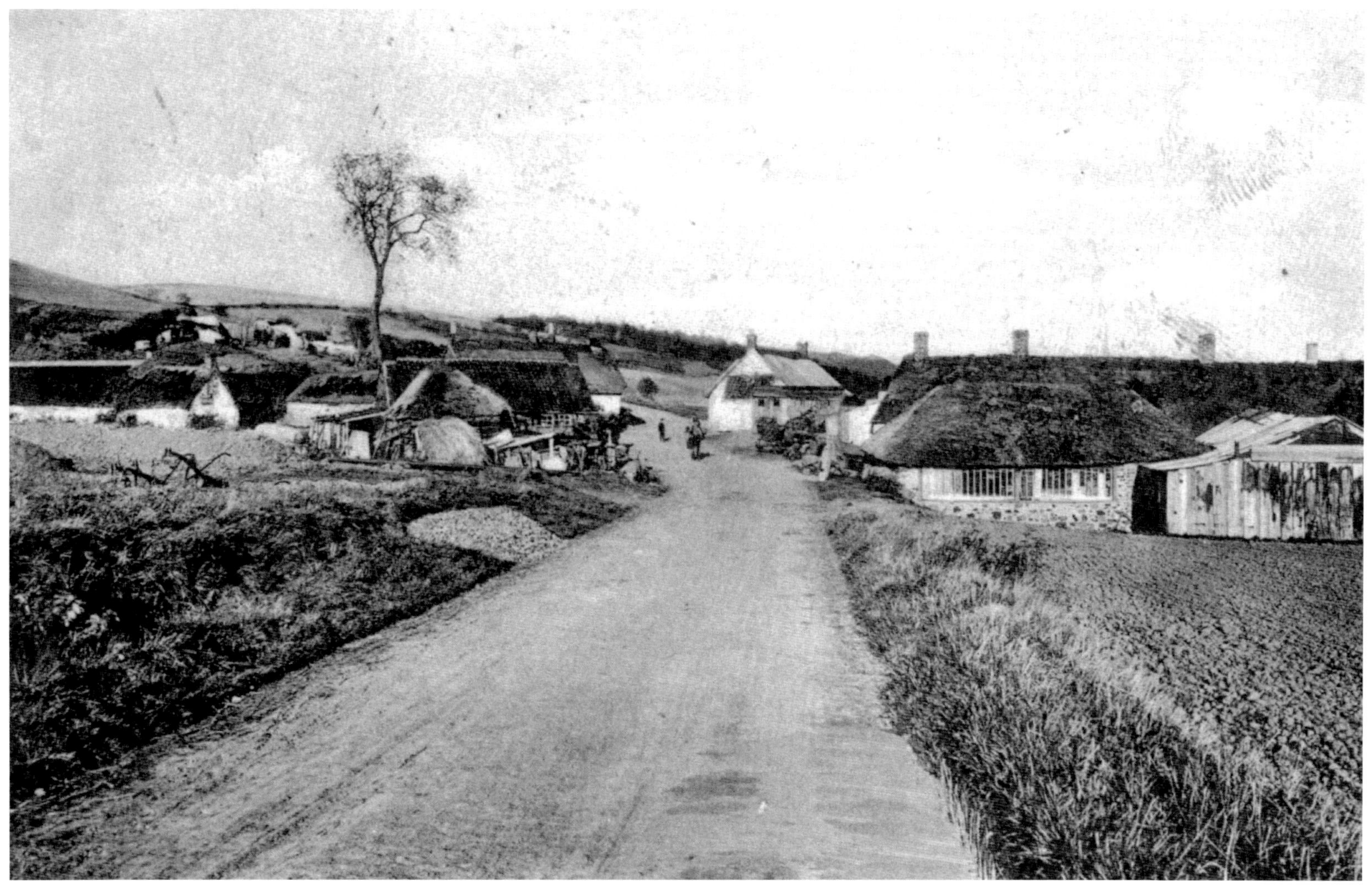

Northwards over the fertile agricultural lands of the Carse are found a series of settlements, each nestling in the valley of a small burn. Pitroddie lies two miles north west of Errol, on the old road which kept to the foot of the Sidlaws, above the treacherous and often flooded Carse lands. This 1905 photograph shows that at that time most cottages had roofs thatched with reed, but most of these have now disappeared.

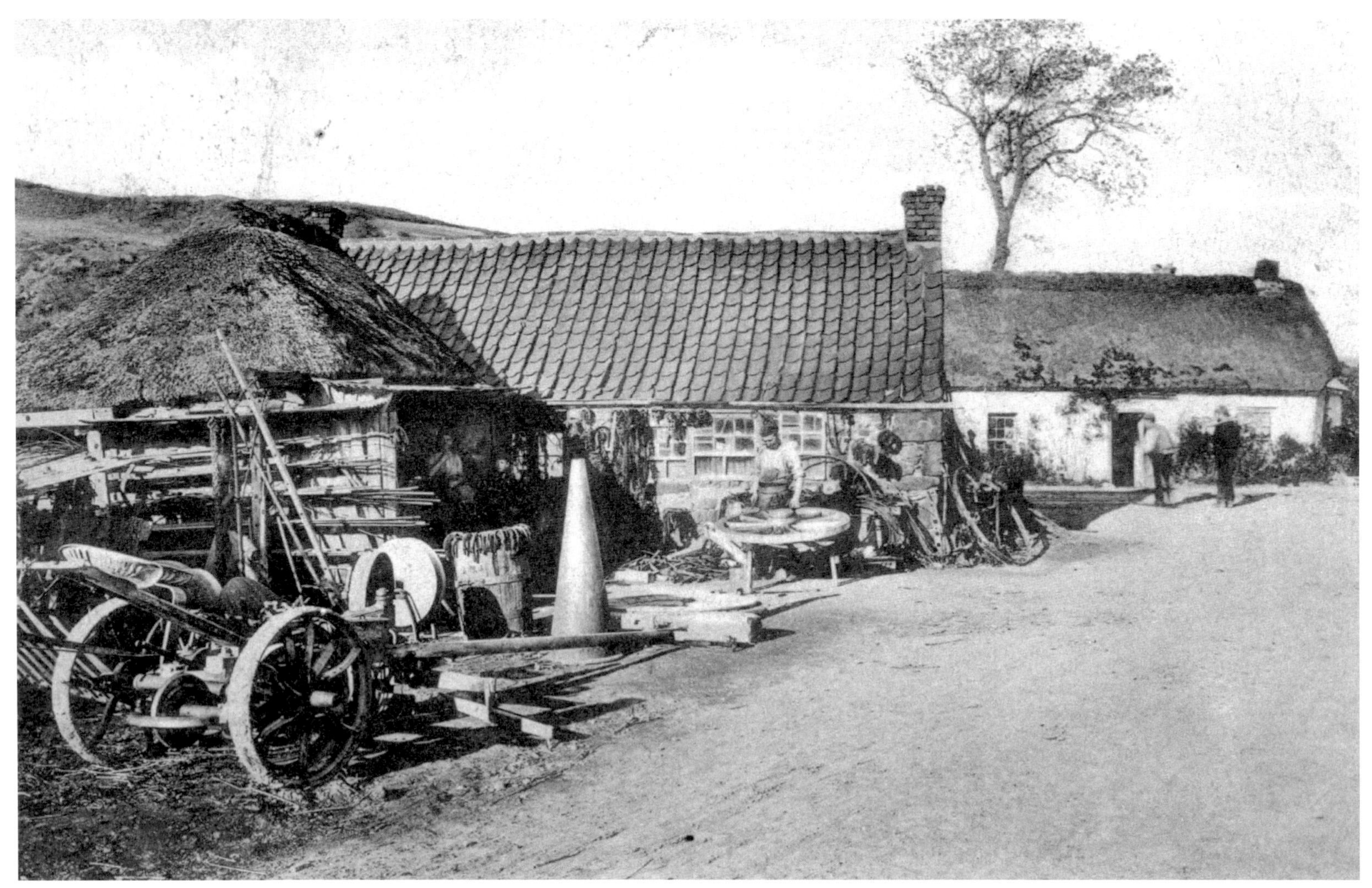

Each village along the length of the Carse, with the heavy dependence on agriculture could, and did, provide enough work to support a smithy. Pitroddie was no exception. Amongst the assorted detritus lie various farm implements, a hand cranked grindstone and a large mandril; the smith is working on a wheel. Several of the buildings still have thatched roofs. Nothing from this scene remains today.

     Pitroddie

Pitroddie Den was home to a quarry working a fine hard-wearing grey whinstone much used for road setts and kerbs in Dundee, and to a lesser extent in Perth. Some quarrymen lived in basic cottages close by the quarry, while others walked each day to and from Errol. The unworked stone was much used for field boundary walls. The quarry was operated by Dundee Police Commissioners from 1858, stone being carted to a siding at Inchcoonans. It closed in 1915. Agates and cornelians are said to have been plentiful in the glen, and legend has it that William Wallace used a cave here as a hide-out!

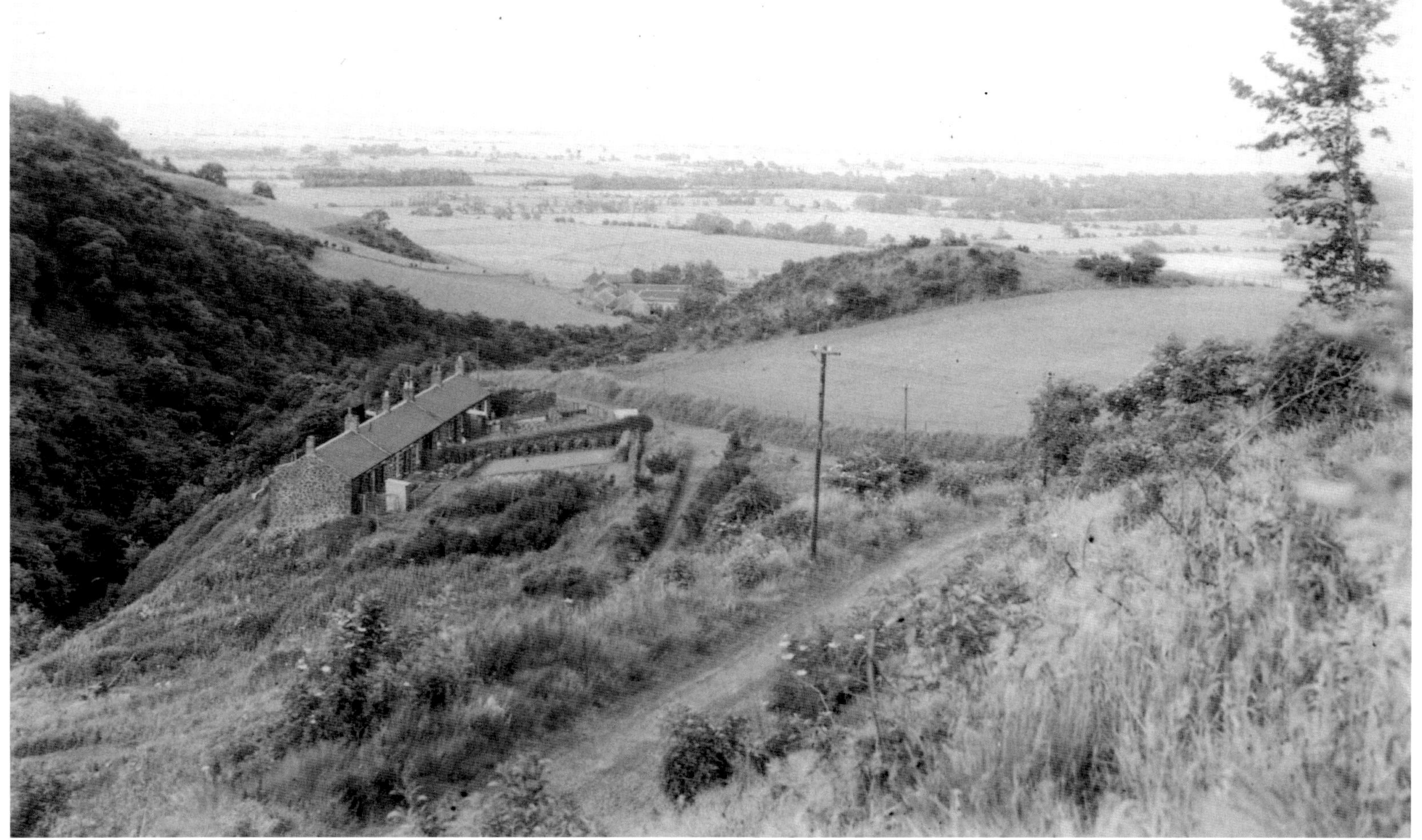

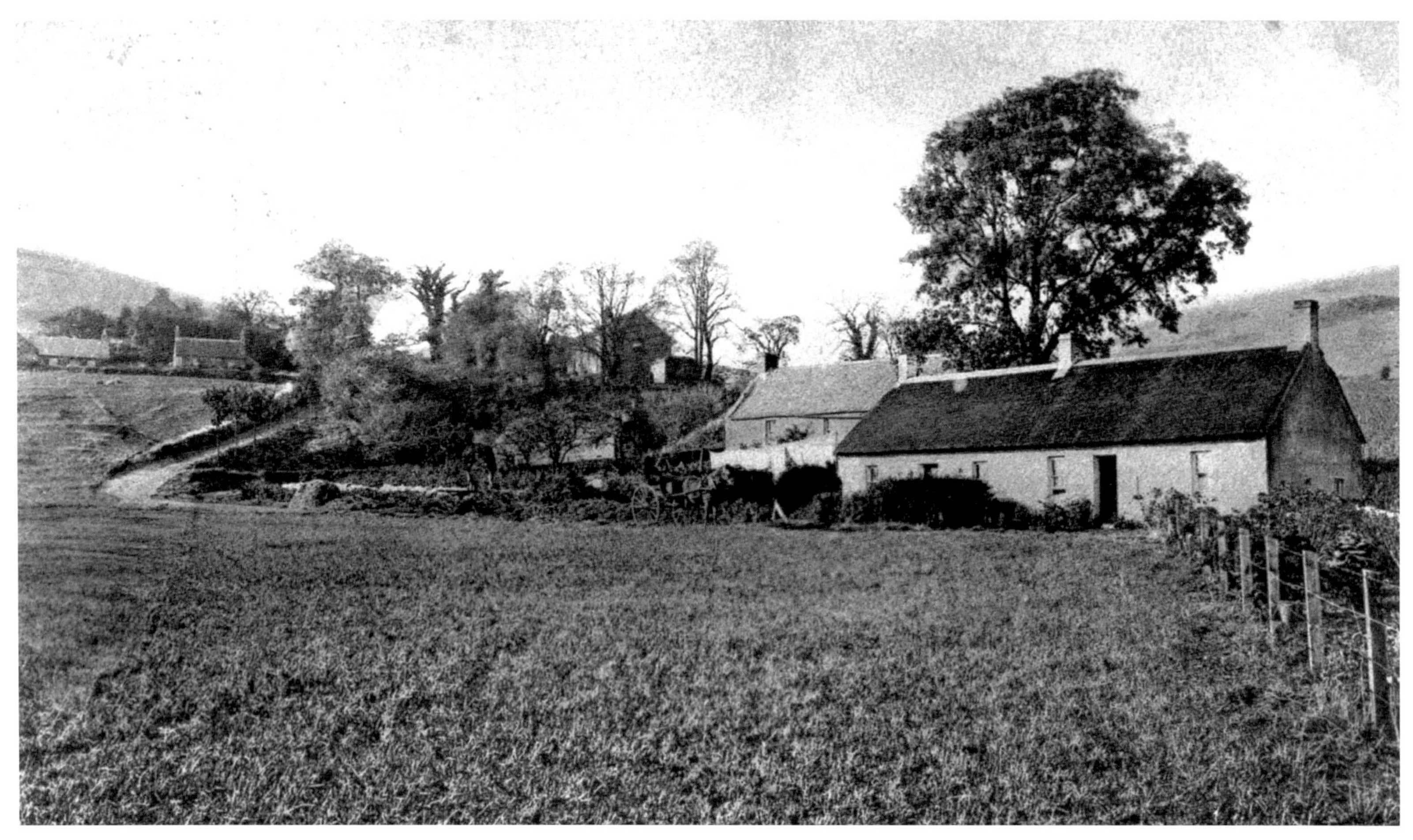

Kilspindie (*above and opposite*) occupies the next small glen to the east, but during the 19th century the population declined and many of the old farm workers' cottages were abandoned. This trend has reversed since the Second World War, the favoured position on the lower slopes of the Sidlaws making the dwellings highly desirable for commuting easily to Dundee and Perth. A prisoner of war camp was built close by and there was a model of Castle Evelick built by Italian Prisoners of War in a garden at Muiredge.

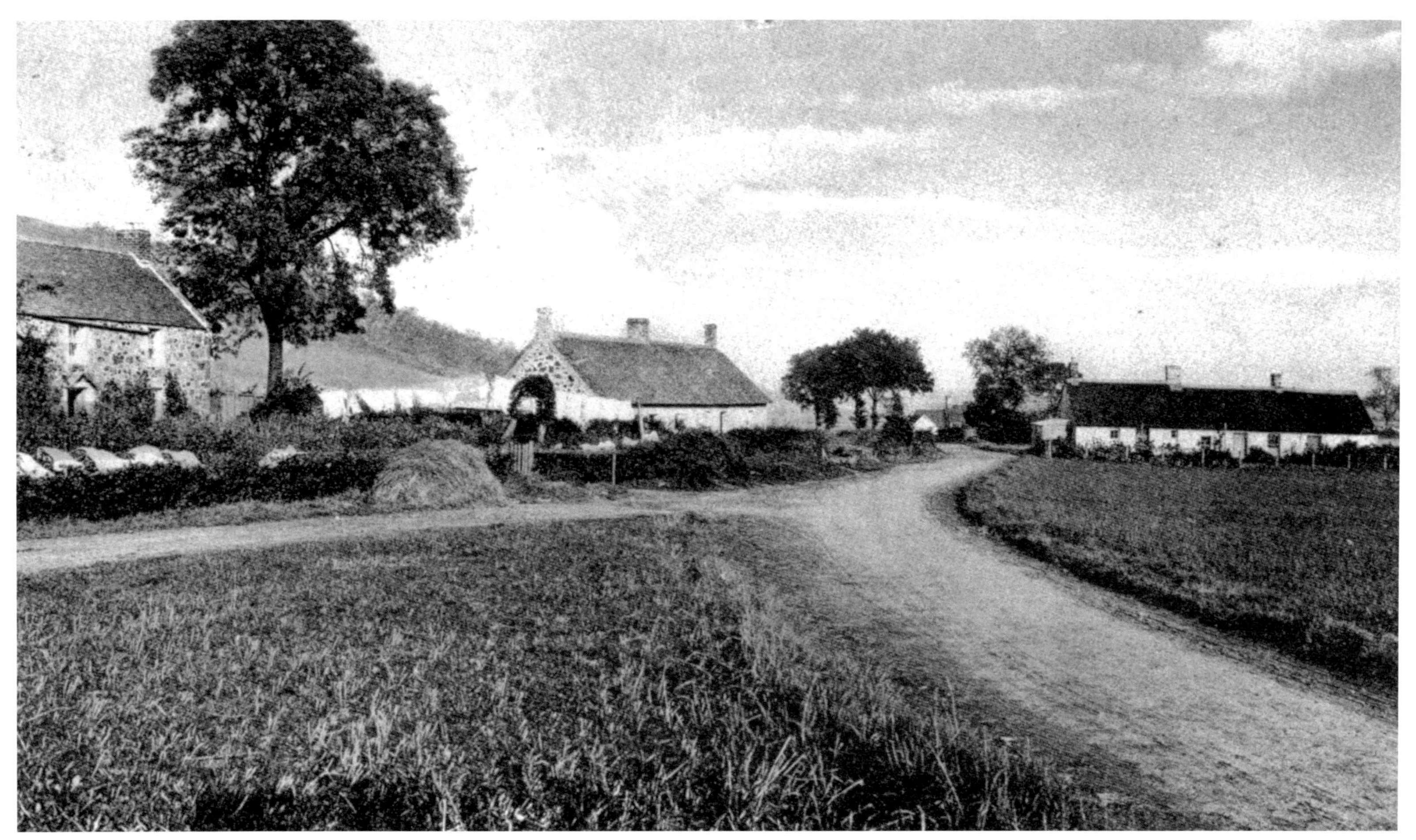

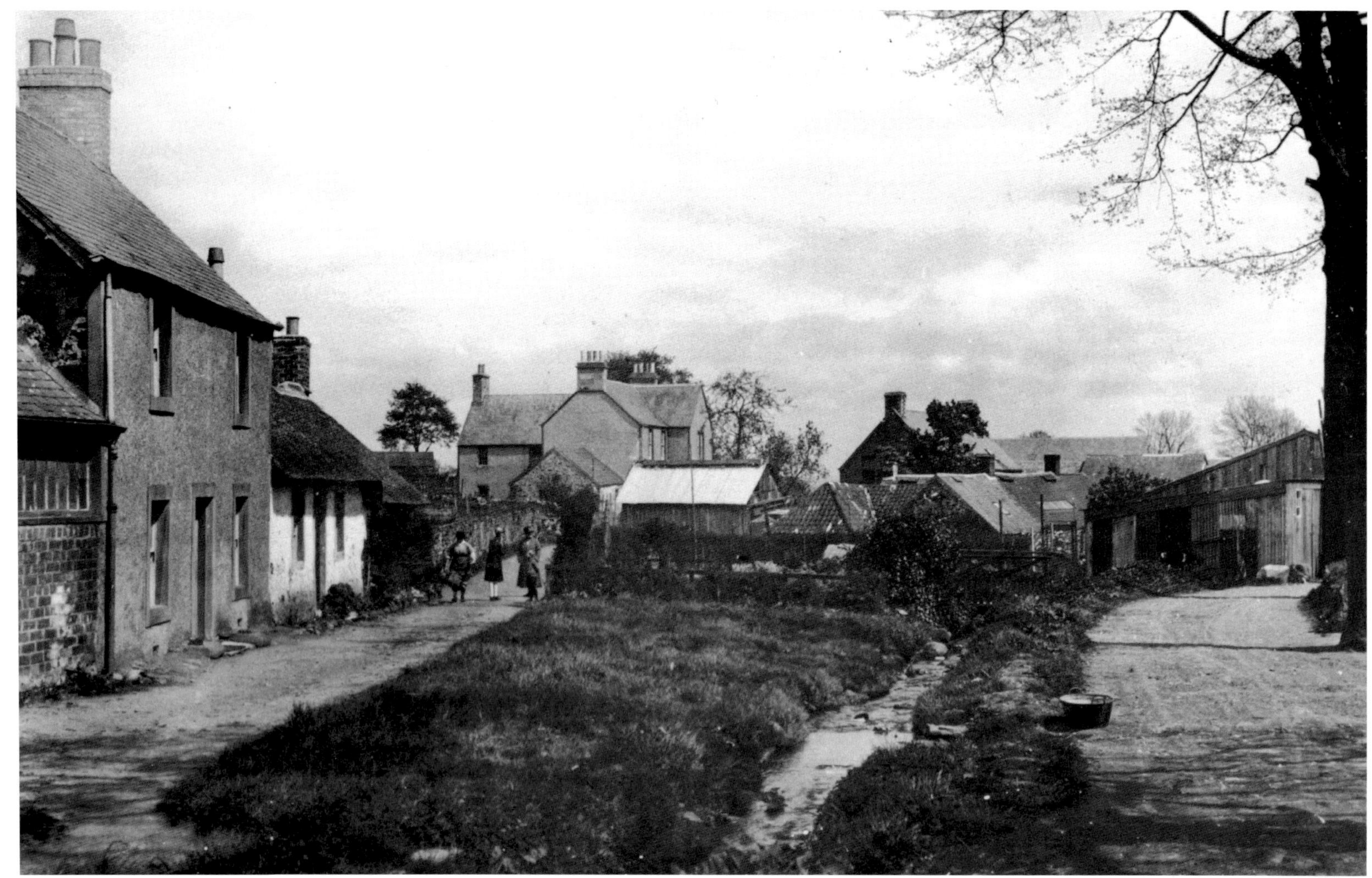

Rait village, looking east, possibly in the early thirties. This was the next village when travelling in an easterly direction along the original Perth to Dundee road before construction of the new turnpike in the latter years of the eighteenth century. Rait is just off a north-south road passing through one of the glens of the Sidlaws, to join the Perth to Coupar Angus road west of Balbeggie. This attractive hamlet, with the burn running through the middle of the village, was a magnet for artists and photographers. The washing tub or bath to the right indicates that good use was probably still being made of the burn.

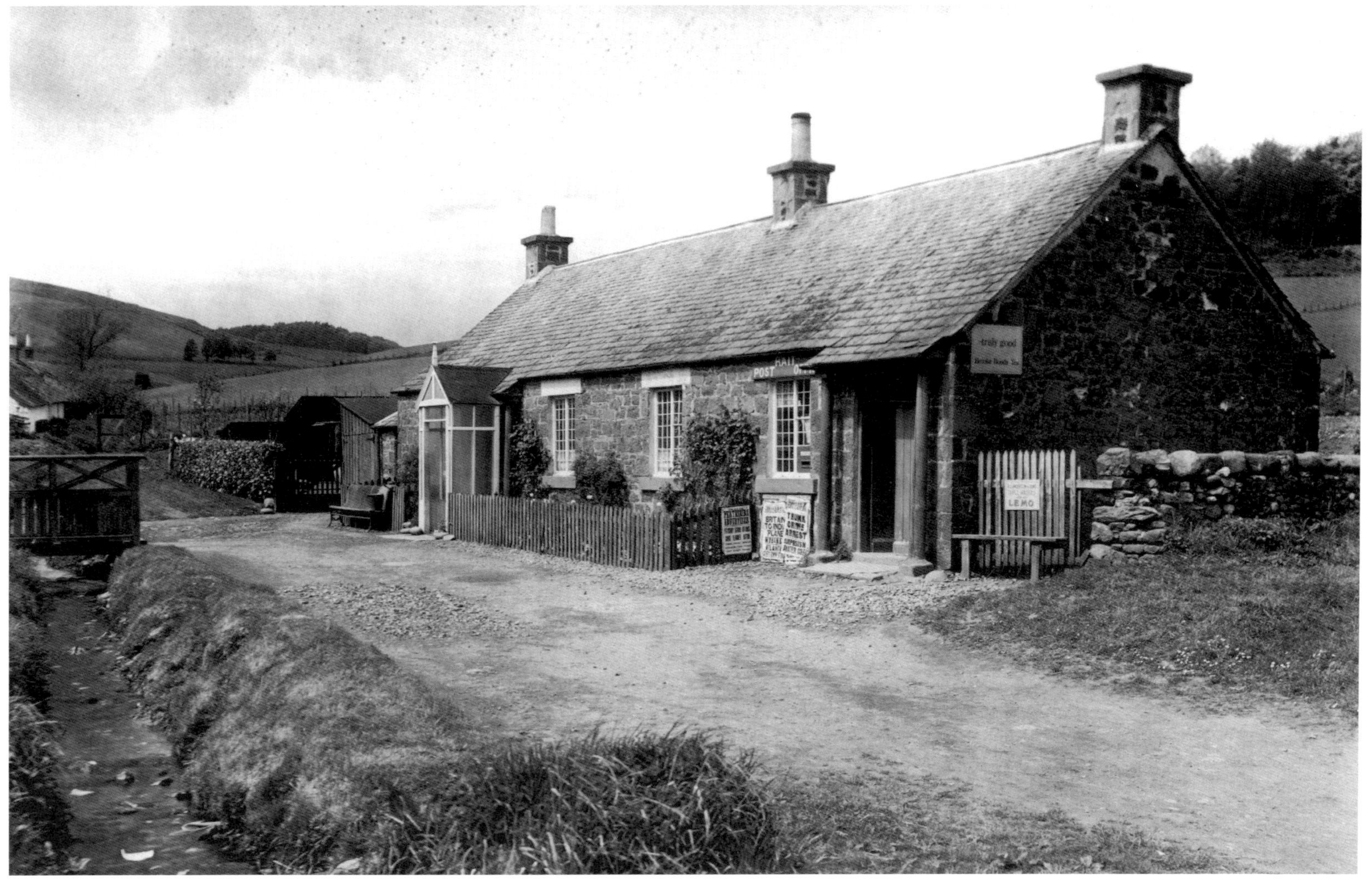

Rait Post Office, with the burn again passing the front door. The photograph can be dated by the newspaper bills alongside the front door. These refer to 'Britain to India Plane wrecked' and 'Trunk crime arrest'. The events referred to took place after the first Imperial Airways flight from London to Karachi in March 1929. No indication then that those rural post offices were anything other than an essential part of the local community.

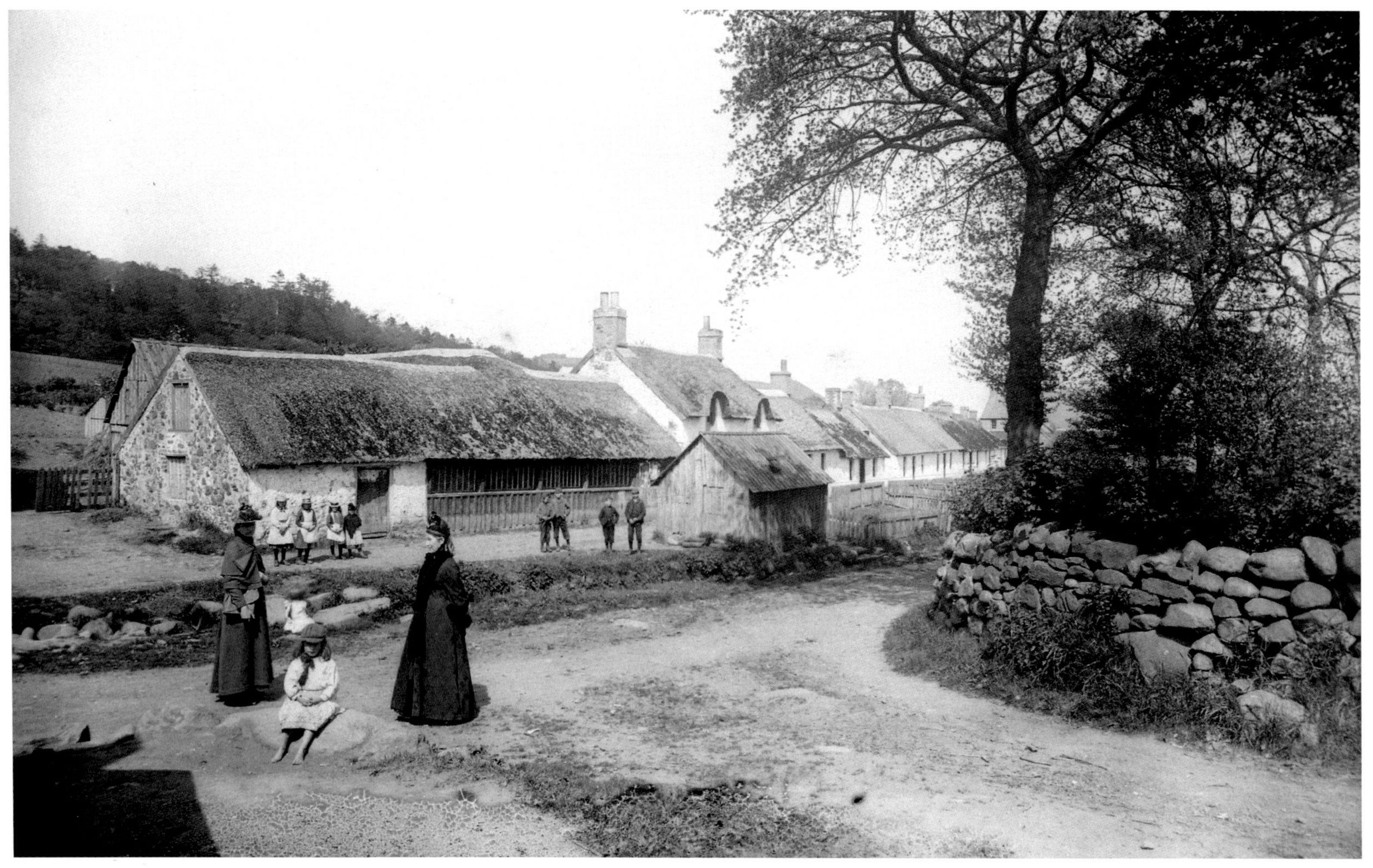

This atmospheric composition of personalities in Rait is by Dundonian Alexander Wilson, taken circa 1900. The buildings have since been converted into cottages and the thatched roofs are now replaced by slate, but the tranquillity remains. Rait is now home to an extremely popular antiques centre. The famous Dundee artist J McIntosh Patrick painted many scenes of the Carse and its farming scenery. One of his finest works was painted in Rait, entitled 'The Three Oaks'; the three oaks remain today as he found and recorded them. [Photo courtesy www.photopolis.org].

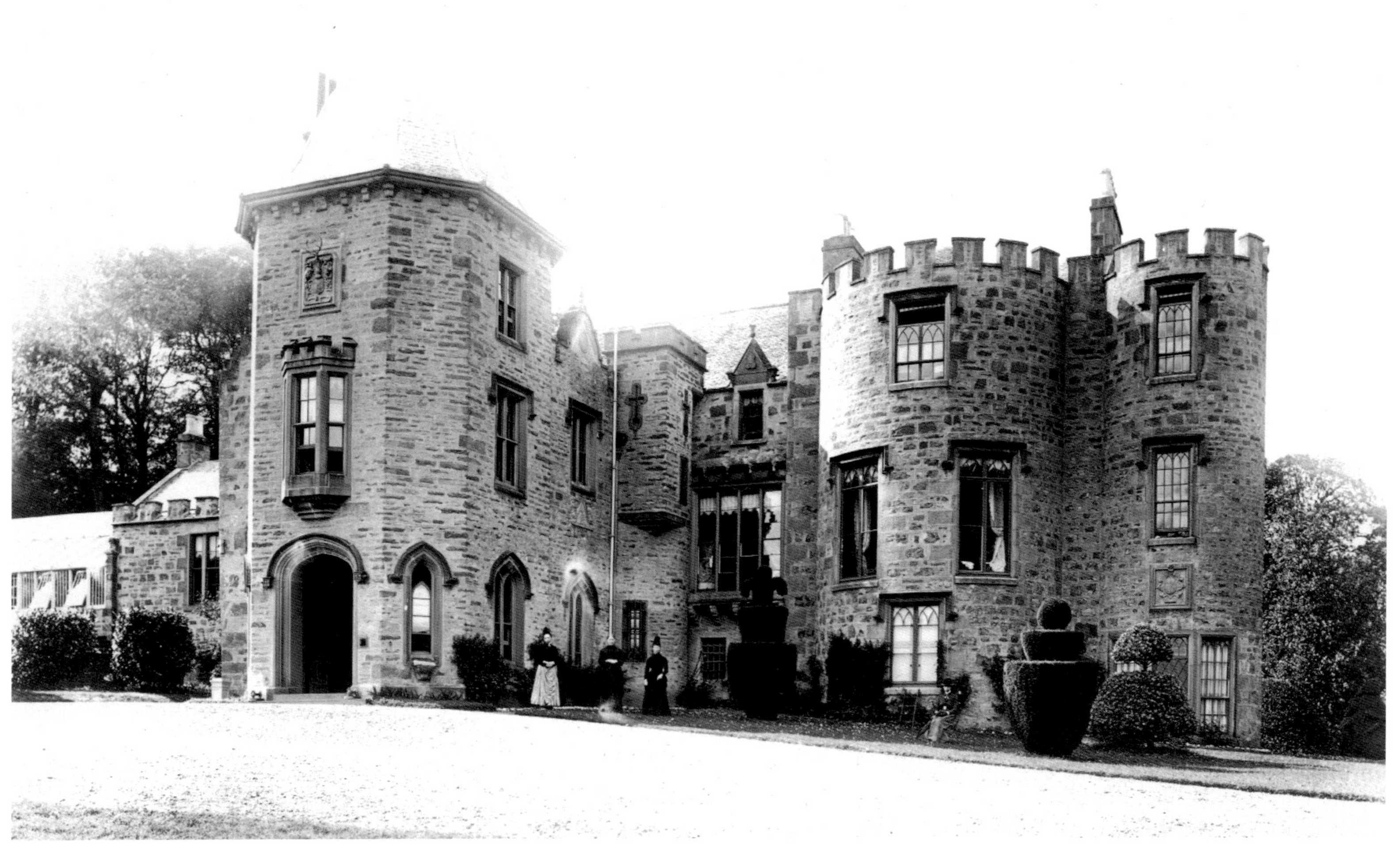

Another of the former fortified houses of the north Carse, Fingask Castle by Rait which has its first mention in the year 1115. The oldest part of the present structure perched on the Braes of the Carse dates back to 1594 and was built for Patrick Bruce. A seat of the Thriepland family since the end of the sixteenth century, the castle has a remarkable historical pedigree, having been visited not only by the Old Pretender 'King James III & VIII' in 1716, but also by the Young Pretender, Bonnie Prince Charlie in 1745. Today it is a very popular and spectacular venue for wedding ceremonies.

Fingask Castle   53

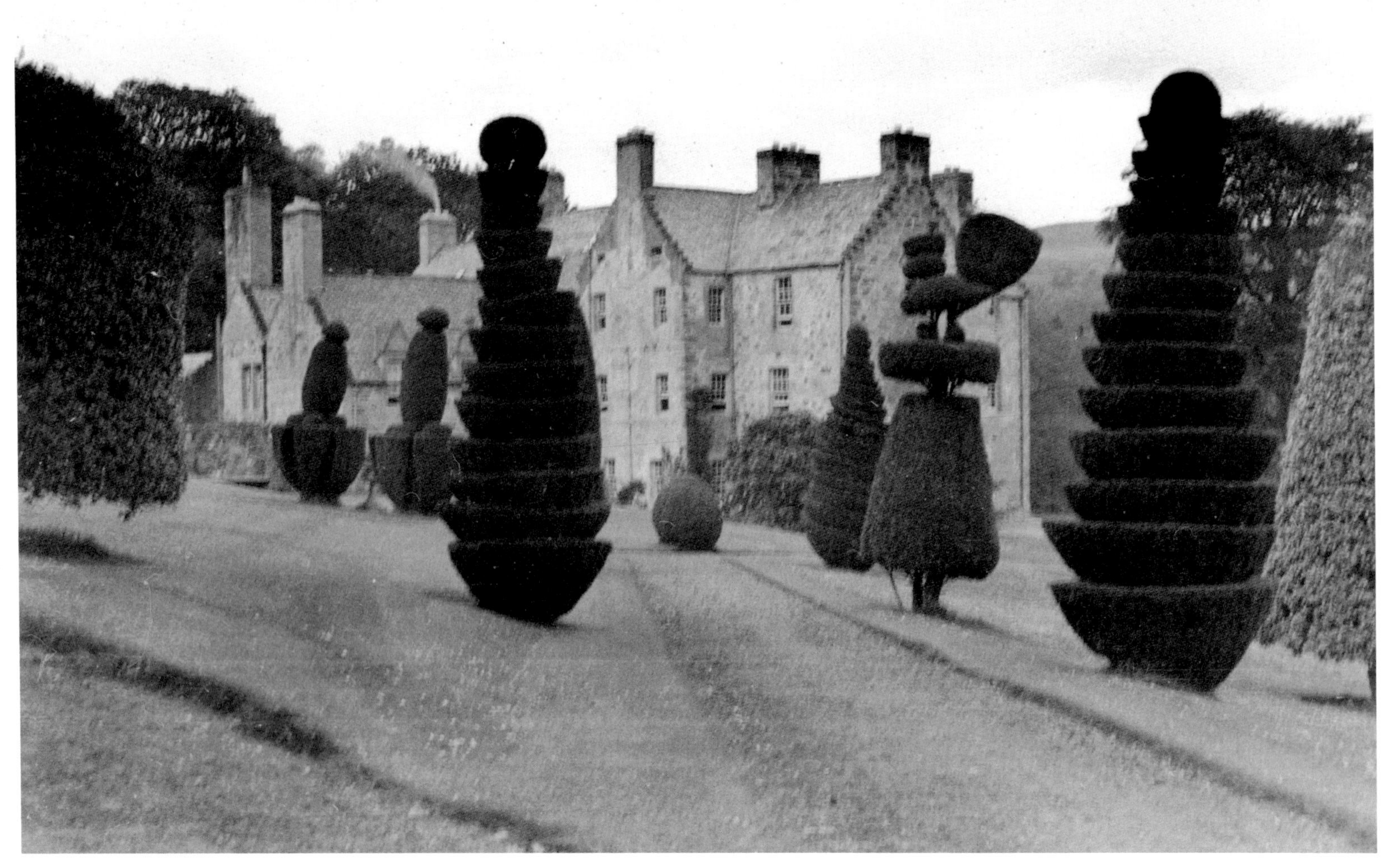

The topiary at Fingask has been a feature of the gardens for many years, the plantings possibly having been commenced by Sir Patrick Thriepland and his wife Eupheme Conqueror in the late seventeenth century. A Victorian description was 'rural picturesque is the style of adornment that prevails'.

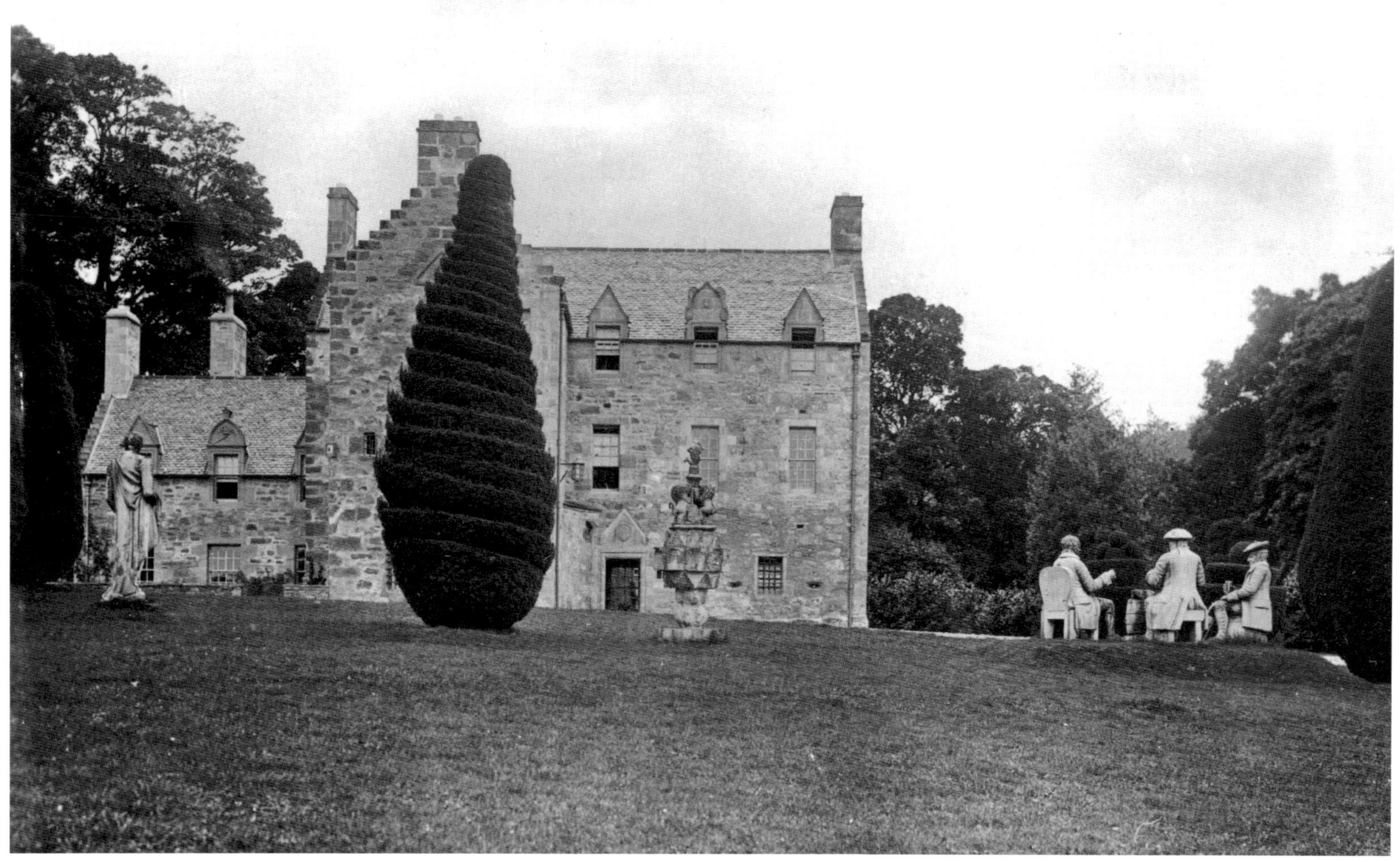

A unique feature of the Fingask gardens is a number of life-size statues, the early 19th century work, it is believed, of Perthshire masons David and William Anderson. Several commemorate the works of Robert Burns and Walter Scott – The Three Beggars, Tam O'Shanter and Flora Macdonald being among the characters portrayed. Typical are the carvings to the right and left in this view, while between is an ancient sundial which is said to have at one time graced Holyrood Palace in Edinburgh.

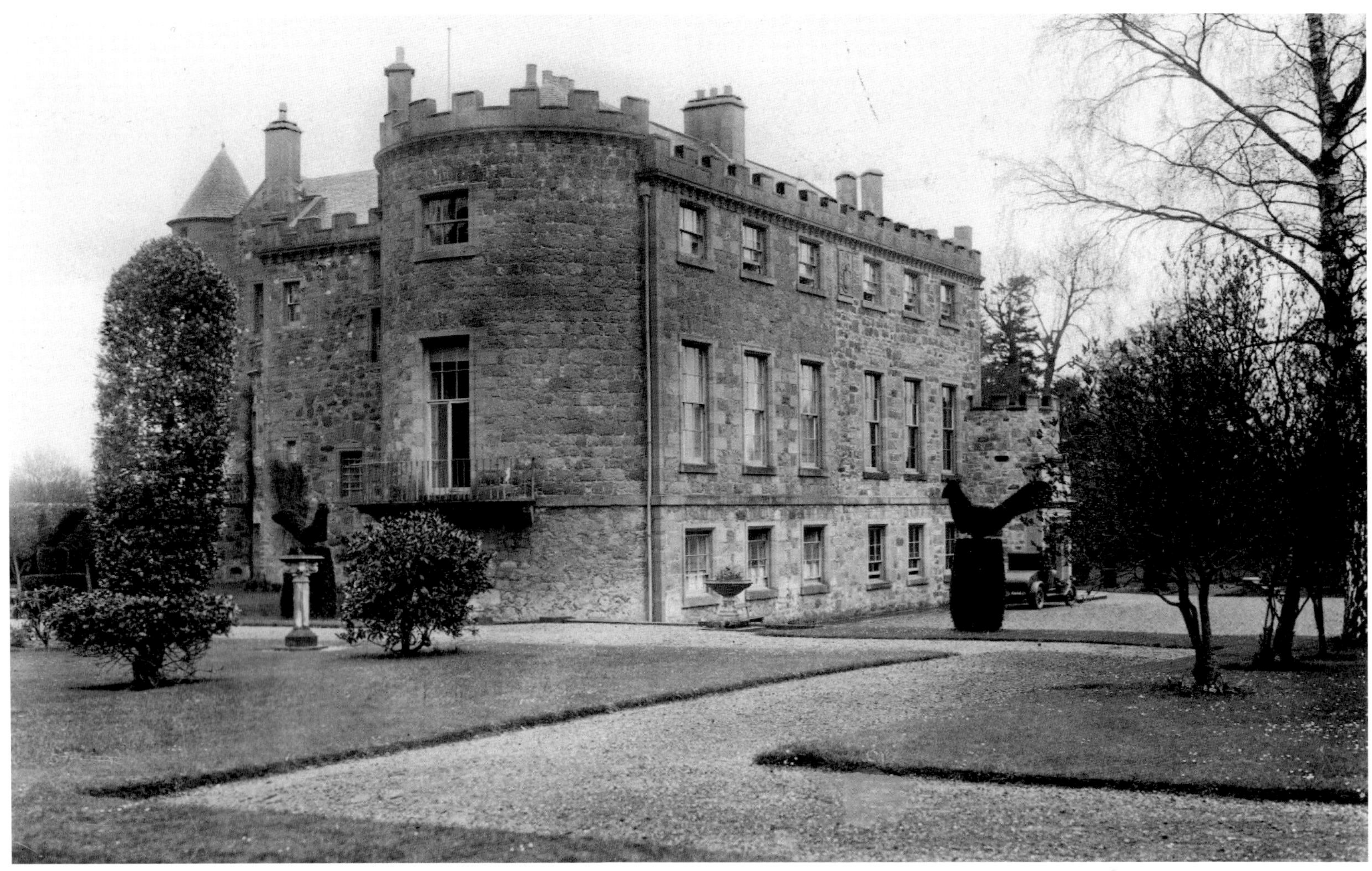

The earliest parts of Megginch Castle, just to the north of Errol, probably date back to the 15th century, when it was built for the Hays of Megginch. Now the seat of the Drummonds of Megginch, Baron Strange, the castle was one of the more memorable settings used in the 1994 film 'Rob Roy'. The red sandstone structure was recorded as early as 1460 and was extended and modified in the ensuing centuries. A fire destroyed a large part of the building in 1969 when a hidden passageway below the drive collapsed under the weight of the fire engine.

        Megginch Castle